51st Indiana Volunteer Infantry Regiment
"The Prisoner, and How Treated"

A YANKEE

IN REBEL

PRISONS

Lt. Alva C. Roach, A. A. D. C.
(Additional Aide-De-Camp)
1865

Copyright 2011 by the Publisher James Keir Baughman, Fort Walton Beach, Florida, for preservation of American history under Federal Legislation pertaining to Literary Public Domain. Manufactured and printed in the United States of America..

ISBN # 978-0-9790443-9-7

www.baughmanliterary.com

All rights reserved. No part of the Version may be reproduced or transmitted by any means, electronic or otherwise, or posted on the Internet without written permission of the Publisher. The edition has been altered and new copyright applies.

While a renewed title far better illustrates the powerful content of his book, Lt. Alva C. Roach's original title page, and the entirety of his words, have been retained exactly as he wrote them in 1865 at the end of America's terrible Civil War.

Original Copyright 1865 by Alva C. Roach and The Railroad City Publishing House, Indianapolis, Indiana. First Edition manufactured and printed in the United States.

THE PRISONER OF WAR, AND HOW TREATED

By Lieutenant A. C. Roach, A. A. D. C.

(1865)

Containing a history of Colonel Streight's expedition to the rear of Bragg's army in the spring of 1863, and a correct account of the treatment and condition of the Union prisoners of war in the Rebel prisons of the South in 1863-4. Being the actual experience of a Union officer during twenty-two months' imprisonment in rebeldom. With personal adventures, biographical sketches, and history of Andersonville prison pen.

Published By

THE RAILROAD CITY PUBLISHING HOUSE,
A. D. Streight, Proprietor.

North-East Corner Washington and Meridian Streets, Indianapolis, Ind. 1865.

Entered according to Act of Congress, in the year one thousand eight hundred and sixty-five, by A. D. STREIGHT, in the Clerk's Office of the District Court of the United States, for the District of Indiana

Hall & Hutchlnson, Stereotypers

PREFACE

The preparation of this work was first contemplated, and partly executed, while I was confined in the rebel prisons of the South; and with the intention of publishing it immediately after my release or escape from captivity.

But the sudden collapse of the military power of the people arrayed in armed rebellion against the Government, following soon there-after, at first determined me to forego the publication of a work, which I conceived might possibly tend to keep alive the embers of discord between us and our Southern foes, and as far as in me lie, consign to oblivion the memory of their wicked deeds, and forget the sufferings and wrongs of myself and fellow captives.

Subsequent events, however, have shown that our late enemies are not possessed of the same spirit of kindly feeling and friendship that we have extended to them. Moreover, that the leaders among them have, under the dissembling guise of *repentance,* sought the pardon and confidence of the nation - which, by force of arms, in four years of bloody war, they failed to dismember - that they might, with the wily arts of the politician, accomplish its destruction.

Believing that subserviency to the demands of those lately leading the armed hosts arrayed against us, by the slave Oligarchy, and the wholesale and indiscriminate pardon extended them by our Chief Magistrate, will, at no distant day, render fruitless the glorious work accomplished by our noble armies, and vain the gallant deeds and heroic sufferings of the brave men of whom they were com-posed, I send forth to the public this volume; which, without pre-tensions to literary merit, breathes the dying moans and starving wails of twenty thousand Union soldiers, whose shroudless and uncoffined bodies moulder beneath the sod, adjacent to the rebel prisons in which they were tortured to death, trusting that whatever influence it may exercise will aid in bringing the guilty leaders of treason to just punishment, for their enormous crimes against humanity.

Without any aspirations whatever, to literary notoriety, I have endeavored to give a plain, unvarnished narrative of facts and incidents of prison life, as they occurred, under my own observation, during twenty-two months in various rebel prisons. I have added, also, the statements of several other Union prisoners, who stand ready to vouch for the same with their affidavits.

In this recital of the terrible woe of our soldiers who were prisoners of war, I do not wish it to be understood that I charge the mass of the Southern people with complicity in the inhuman treatment they received. Jeff Davis, Robert E. Lee, and other rebels high in authority, and the monster's whom they placed in immediate command of the prisoners, are alone responsible, and on their heads let just and condign punishment fall.

A. C. R.

CONTENTS

CHAPTER I

COLONEL STREIGHT'S EXPEDITION

Introductory Remarks - Organization of Streight's Expedition - Departure from Nashville-Palmyra, Tennessee - Experience with Mules - Foraging Parties – Tuscumbia - Eastport - Disastrous Affair - Loyal Citizens - Battle of Day's Gap - Rebel Barbarities - Battle of Crooked Creek – Capture of Doctor King – Ambushing the Enemy.

CHAPTER II

STREIGHT'S EXPEDITION CONTINUED

Burning Black Creek Bridge - A Rebel Heroine - Battle of Blunt's Farm - Death of Colonel Hathaway - Prospects of Success - Lose the Route - Captain Russell's Party - Surrender to General Forrest.

CHAPTER III

IMPRISONMENT

Rome, Georgia – Arrival at Libby Prison - Description of The Libby - Union Ladies Insulted - Fourth of July in Libby - Stars and Stripes in Prison - Their Capture.

CHAPTER IV

LIFE IN PRISON

Increasing Barbarities - Colonel Streight's Letter to the Rebel Secretary of War - Perfidy of Union Officers - Lieutenant Colonel Sanderson's Communications to the Rebel Commissary - Indignation of the Prisoners - Starved to Death - Escape of a Dead Yankee.

CHAPTER V

BELLE ISLE

Prisoners Compelled to Eat Dog Flesh - The Chickamauga Prisoners - Rebel Hospitals - The Richmond Examiner - It Counsels Murder - Treatment of Rebel Prisoners in the North.

CHAPTER VI

WINTER IN LIBBY

Terrible Suffering - Inside View of Libby - Prisoners Cooking Their Rations - Amusements - Prisoners' Letters - Fresh Fish - Exchange - Night in Libby.

CHAPTER VII

ESCAPE OF ANDERSON AND SKELTON

Preparation for the Escape - Discovered by the Guard - Second Attempt - Final Exit from Richmond - Friendliness of the Slaves - Union Soldiers - Liberty and the Old Flag - The Council of Five - First Escape of Colonel Streight - His Letter to General Meredith - General Morgan's Visit to Libby.

CHAPTER VIII

THE LIBBY TUNNEL

The Negroes in Libby - One Hundred and Nine Officers Escape - Colonel Streight Gets Fast in the Tunnel - Names of the Principal Officers who Escaped - Colonel Streight Secreted by a Loyal Woman Several Days in Richmond - Detectives Searching for Him - Perilous Adventures of the Escaped Prisoners – Safe Arrival in the Union Lines.

CHAPTER IX

KILPATRICK'S EXPEDITION

Attempt to Release the Prisoners - Death of Colonel Dahlgren - Horrible Mutilation of His Body - Plot to Blow Up the Prison - Removal from Libby - Macon - Captain Tabb - A Union Officer Murdered.

CHAPTER X.

GENERAL STONEMAN'S RAID

Stoneman's Cavalry Approach Macon - The Fight and Repulse – Capture of Stoneman and His Command - Removal from Macon - Charleston - Its Desolation - The Work House - Jail - Bombardment of the City - Removal to Columbia - Camp Sorghum.

CHAPTER XI.

ESCAPE OF CAPTAIN RUSSELL

First Attempt - Liberty or Death - Accidental Meeting with a Friend - Long Fasting and Extreme Fatigue – He Makes a Foray on a Flock of Sheep – Recaptured - Lexington Jail - Second Attempt - Receive Aid from the Negroes - Narrow Escape from Drowning - Raw Corn His Only Subsistence - Arrival Inside of Sherman's Lines - Secretary Stanton.

CHAPTER XII

PRISON LIFE AT COLUMBIA

Removal from Camp Sorghum - Asylum Prison - Chandler's String Band - Sherman's March to the Sea - Fall of Savannah and the Encouragement it Gave the Prisoners - Preparations for Escape - Removal from Columbia.

CHAPTER XIII.

ESCAPE OF THE AUTHOR

Out of the Jaws of Death - Recapture of Lieutenant Pool – Ash Cake for General Sherman - Captain Aigan Left Exhausted on the Road - The Slave "Math" - Union Family Near Columbia, South Carolina - Their Kindness to Escaped Prisoners.

CHAPTER XIV

THE OLD FLAG AND LIBERTY

Math Proposes to Steal His Master's Mules - Devastation by Sherman's Army of South Carolina - Concealment at the House of Mr. Carman - The Two Misses

Carman - Change of Base - Luckless Adventure of Captain Aigan - Safe with the Union Army – Lieutenant Colonel Morrow and Captain Rosser - The Ninety Second Ohio Volunteers - Sherman's Bummers - Bummers Report - Arrival at Fayetteville, North Caroline.

CHAPTER XV

ANDERSONVILLE PRISONERS

Horrible Sights in the Streets of Charleston - Our Returned Prisoners at Wilmington - Report of Doctor J. C. Dalton - General Winder and Captain Wertz - Statement of an Andersonville Prisoner.

CHAPTER XVI

ANDERSONVILLE CONTINUED

Eight Months in the Pen - Statement of H. M. Roach - Three Days Without Food of Any Kind - Trading Dead Men for Wood - Letter from Miss Clara Barton - Two Hundred and Sixty-seven Prisoners Wantonly Murdered - Letter from a Georgia Planter.

CHAPTER XVII

PERSONAL SKETCHES

Major Harry White - Captain Driscoll and Lieutenant Pavey - Lieutenant Von Braiday - Captains Flinn and Sawyer – Lieutenant Edwin Read - Major B. C. G. Reed.

COVER PAINTING

"Washington Artillery of New Orleans"

By Don Troiani

DON TROIANI is a soul lost in time; a twentieth century artist to whom the life of the common soldier of the Civil War through the mid Eighteenth Century is as familiar and vivid as the surroundings of his Connecticut studio. While there are many other painters who have turned their attention to historical art, none have done so with the enthusiasm, insight and dedication of this insightful recorder of drama and detail.

In the spirit of presenting historical truth through art, Don Troiani has personally set uncompromising standards of excellence and authenticity in his field that few others can equal. Models are chosen with the greatest care to achieve the proper look of the men in Colonial and Victorian America. The garb and gear of each figure are painstakingly researched. Appropriate backgrounds are found and studied, sometimes sending the artist hundreds of miles from home to examine battlefields and structures firsthand

"If an historical painting is not reasonably accurate, then it's worthless both as art and as a historical document," Troiani declares. "If you are going to become involved in this field then there is little excuse for a pattern of inaccuracies."

Indeed, Troiani's lifelong focus on America's military heritage enables him to present that subject with a credibility that surpasses his contemporaries. For a quarter century, as an expert researcher, he has methodically built one of the great private artifact collections of Civil War, 1812 and Revolutionary War, World War II uniforms, equipage, insignia and weapons which he calls on to add the unique dimension of realism he is so well known for.

Hollywood has enlisted him as consultant on "Civil War Uniforms and Equipage" for the acclaimed feature film "Cold Mountain" starring Nicole Kidman, Rene Zellweger and Jude Law for which he received screen credit. Also in "Cold Mountain, The Journey from Book to Film." Troiani has also been military advisor (and made appearances) on the A&E and History Channel's "Civil Journal" and the miniseries "The American Revolution". Television appearances on "Missing Reward," "Incurable Collector", and "Hunt for Amazing Treasures" are among his credits.

Because of his extensive knowledge of military artifacts, Troiani is regularly contacted by major museums and collectors from across the country who greatly value his firsthand experience. His artifacts have been loaned for the exhibition at the Smithsonian Institution, Delaware Historical Society, Connecticut Museum of History, Pamplin Park, The West Point Museum, Virginia Historical Society and the National Park Service Visitors Center in Gettysburg, PA.

Troiani's artwork has appeared on television productions on NBC,CPTV,CNN, America Online, the A&E, Military and Discovery channels and in uncounted prestigious publications including "The Washington Post", "The Washington Times," "US News and World Reports," "American Heritage," "American Rifleman," "Civil War Times," The Arizona Republic, "America's Civil War", and many others.

Troiani has also authored or co-authored "Don Troiani's Civil War", "Soldiers in America 1754-1865," "Military Buttons of the American Revolution," and "Don Troiani's Regiments and Uniforms of the Civil War", in addition to numerous articles on military artifacts.

Born in New York City in 1949, Troiani's future as a premier interpreter of history seemed predestined. His father, an accomplished commercial artist, encouraged his talented son and kept him supplied with paper, paint and direction. His mother, a successful antiques dealer, nurtured her son's interest in the past and showed him the importance of having a three-dimensional view of history. By the time he began perfecting his skills at the Pennsylvania Academy Of Fine Arts and New York City's Art Students League, his role as a consummate realist was already clear.

Since launching his professional career before the Bicentennial and demonstrating his gift for combining art and historical integrity, there has been a strong, increasing demand for Troiani's work by both distinguished private collectors and important institutions. His work is represented in the collections of museums such as Smithsonian Magazine and the Smithsonian's Museum of History and Technology, Gettysburg NHP, U.S. Army War College, U.S. Marine Corps Museum, Command General Staff College, Ft. Leavenworth, KS, The Charleston Museum, North Carolina Museum of History, the Pentagon, U.S. Army National Guard Bureau, West Point Museum, U.S. Cavalry Museum at Fort Riley Kansas, and the National Civil War Museum, Harrisburg. PA.

In 1995 he designed the three Civil War battlefield commemorative coins for the United States Mint. His work has also appeared on a U.S. postal card commemorating the 350th anniversary of the U.S. National Guard. Troiani is also a recipient of the "Meritorious Service to America" award.

Epiologue, 145 Years After

This fascinating work by Lt Alva C. Roach, completed and published in the year 1865, is surely one of the most descriptive of many personal journals written during the years of America's terrible Civil War. We are delighted to be able to re-publish it.

We employed Lt. Roach's words, his eyewitness accounts, in a number of incidents remembered in our book "The Boys From Lake County," a history of the 73rd Indiana Volunteer Infantry Regiment. Lt. Roach, with his Regiment, the 51st Indiana Volunteer's, fought alongside the 73rd Indiana in two major engagements, notably the several, running, battles of the week-long Raid of Streight's Brigade in April and May of 1863.

We are grateful to have been able to cite what he saw and experienced, simply because Lt Roach's descriptions of everything around him are so complete and compelling as to make the reader feel as though we were there with him and our forefathers.

Lt Roach's book is uncommon in another way. He declared his work unvarnished truth, and much appears so. Yet, his words ring constantly with far more, oozing a remarkable hatred and vilification toward Americans of the South. In fact, he often refers to them sneeringly as "the chivalry." In virtually every page Roach proclaims Southerners as traitors, murderers, fiends, villains, and robbers...rather than as they were, devoted Americans who dearly loved this Nation and its freedoms, for which they were the major founding force. It was a view which flourished in the North, but far less often was expressed in such offensive terms.

Without critique of individual incidents described, our twenty-five years of research tells us that it now does not seem generally true that war-time POW prisons in the North were better managed in regard to comfort, food, or care than in the South. Most studies we reviewed indicate that prisoners on both sides were treated about equally. Obviously, though, individual situations surely must have brought about varying levels of care at certain times. Perhaps such incidents are what Lt Roach chose to write about. Clearly, as he states, Union officers imprisoned with him testified that Southern prison care and food was, at least, adequate. In Libby prison, for instance, Lt Roach writes that some imprisoned Union officers were too well fed to fit in the escape tunnel. Moreover, our research seems to show that prisoner care, especially in regard to food, was generally equal to or better than soldiers in the field on both sides.

No doubt, however, Andersonville prison was an unparalleled Southern disaster with a great many deaths. It is fact, though, that Andersonville occurred late in the Civil War at a time in which Confederate resources, even to feed its own troops, were near exhaustion. Sherman's march to the sea and his slash and burn attacks on private farms and herds had even further lessened available food in the South. But the greatest cause of prisoner deaths on both sides was that Gen Ulysses S. Grant had stopped all prisoner exchanges with the goal of preventing them from going back into battle and hence shortening the War by starving the South for troops. If all those men…of both sides…had been back home or back in their own Regiments, prisons would have been far less necessary.

As a writer who had grandfathers in both the Union and Confederate armies, it must be recalled that Southerners of 1861 were far from "traitors." It is little remembered today, but before Lincoln's determination to War, Southerners were peacefully in the process of separating from a new federal administration which seemed determined to shrink freedoms and bring about big government control in patent opposition to the visions of our Founding Fathers.

145 years after the end of the Civil War, a great many Americans see that effort continuing at warp speed toward big government, Communist-like, domination of individual freedoms, America's free enterprise system, and State's rights which were designed by our Founding Fathers to protect America from just such a calamity.

In fact, by the time Lincoln's War began, Southerners were far along the path toward independence, having assumed authority peacefully over most federal offices and facilities in the South, having already organized and established their new, profoundly Constitutional, governing.

So…here is a caution. If your heritage is of Southern origin you may find Lt. Roach's condemnation quite disconcerting, even while reveling in his powerful, eyewitness-to-history description.

In this Year of Our Lord 2011…it seems no longer that "Rebels" reside just in the "South." Americans who completely fathom and believe deeply in the original words of our Constitution, and the ideas of our Founding Fathers, (opposite the prosperity-less, murderous, devastation of big government, Communist-like, control) are found in every State, in every region, in every dialect, of America. And they are speaking out again…loudly… in favor of individual freedom.

James Keir Baughman

A Yankee in Rebel Prisons

Chapter I

INTRODUCTORY REMARKS

When new arrivals of unfortunate prisoners were ushered into the gloomy precincts of the various rebel prisons of the South, by the brutal and inhuman officials in charge, they were almost invariably addressed by the old inhabitants with the simple but important interrogatory, "Where were YOU captured?"

Consequently, knowing the propensity of my old comrades and fellow prisoners to learn where and how each individual prisoner was "gobbled," I shall, in the first place, although it does not properly belong to the original design of our history of prison life, give a sketch of Colonel Streight's expedition to Georgia in the spring of 1863, when, it will be recollected, his entire command, consisting of about twelve hundred men and one hundred officers, were made prisoners of war, and charged with such heinous crimes by the then exultant, and seemingly triumphant and successful rebels, that their authorities refused to exchange us, on any terms whatever. This action of the rebel officials at once put a stop to the workings of the cartel arranged some months previous, for the immediate exchange of all prisoners of war, as soon as practicable after their capture. This, then, being the beginning of that premeditated and systematic plan of inhuman treatment, starvation and murder, practiced by the rebel authorities during the last two years of the war, on Union soldiers who fell into their hands, I trust is sufficient apology for introducing it into this work.

ORGANIZATION of STREIGHT'S EXPEDITION

The spring of 1863 opened with the prospect of being a season of inactivity for the Army of the Cumberland. The rebel General Bragg, with a large and well equipped army, occupied near

A Yankee in Rebel Prisons

Tullahoma, Tennessee, a strong natural position, improved by all the ingenuity known to military science, until it was almost impregnable. Consequently it was not in the progamme of the cautious and sagacious Rosecrans, then commanding the Army of the Cumberland, to make an advance movement until his command was in a condition of health, numbers and equipments, that certain and decisive victory would be inevitable. These important military items it was not expected could be brought about before, perhaps, the middle of the approaching summer.

To the mind of Colonel A. D. Streight, of the Fifty-First Indiana Volunteer Infantry, this term of inaction was a period of *ennui*, and afforded the enemy in his stronghold at Tullahoma a rest and feeling of security, that his active and restless spirit could not contemplate. He therefore made application to the commanding General for an independent mounted brigade, a command of this descripttion necessarily affording an opportunity for constant and active service; and would, if directed in the proper manner, draw from the banks of the Cumberland and Ohio the guerrilla bands of Forrest, Morgan and other noted chieftains in the rebel service, and give them employment in their own boasted land of "Dixie."

This enterprise of Colonel S. was favorably received by General Rosecrans, and the following named troops accordingly placed under his command and designated as the INDEPENDENT PROVISIONAL BRIGADE, designed for special secret service: His own regiment, (the Fifty-First Indiana;) Third Ohio, Colonel O. A. Lawson; Seventy-Third Indiana, Colonel Gilbert Hathaway; and Eightieth Illinois, Lieutenant Colonel A, F. Rodger's commanding; also companies D and E of the First Middle Tennessee cavalry,

A Yankee in Rebel Prisons

commanded by Captain D. D. Smith. Active preparations were at once commenced for an expedition to Alabama and Georgia, for the purpose of destroying the vast supplies of the rebels and the railroad communication in the interior of those States.

On arriving at the city of Nashville, where Colonel Streight was ordered to fit out his command, preparatory to starting on the expedition, he organized the following staff, to·wit: Captain D. L. ·Wright, Fifty-First Indiana Volunteers, to be A. A. A. G.; Major W. L. Peck, Third Ohio, to be Brigade Surgeon; Lieutenant J. G, Doughty, Regimental Quarter-master Fifty-First Indiana Volunteers, to be A. A. Q. M,; Captain E. M. Driscoll, Third Ohio Volunteers, to be A. A. I. G.; Lieutenant C. W. Pavey, Eightieth Illinois Volunteers, to be Brigade Ordnance Officer; and Lieutenant A. C. Roach, Fifty-First Indiana Volunteer's to be A. D, C.

Operations now commenced in earnest, Colonel Streight and the officers of his staff working day and night to supply the command with the necessary clothing, ordnance and equipments for the expedition; and at the end of the third day, with the exception of the requisite number of animals to mount the command, the "Provisional Brigade" was thoroughly organized and equipped, officers and men ready and anxious for any duty they might be called upon to perform.

DEPARTURE FROM NASHVILLE

On the afternoon of April tenth Colonel Streight received orders from General Garfield, Chief of Staff, to embark at once, on steamers then at the landing, and proceed down the river to Palmyra; everything was speedily put on board and got in readiness for starting; and on the morning of the 11th, from the decks of the transports chartered for our expedition, as they sped irresistibly along before the mighty force of the river's current and power of the steam engine, we took a farewell view of the Capital of "Old Tennessee," and soon the church spires and cupolas, reflecting the beams of the morning sun, were lost to the eye, and the ragged banks of the Cumberland, and the spiral columns of white steam ascending from the exhaust pipes of the numerous boats composing our fleet., and forming behind us, over vale and hill, a milky track of the circuitous course of the Cumberland, were the only objects to divert the mind or attract the attention, until we arrived at the place which, in the palmy days of peace, was pointed out to the traveler on the now classic waters of the Cumberland, as the village of Palmyra, but now only a heap of black and charred ruins; presenting one of the many scenes of devastation that will tell, for years to come, that our country was once convulsed with one of the most unnatural and gigantic wars of any age - a war inaugurated by a. people whose sole aim and object was to rear an autocratic government on the ruins of constitutional liberty and human freedom.

LANDING AT PALMYRA

At this place our command disembarked and bivouacked for the night. Early the next morning a detail of four companies was placed under command of Colonel Lawson, of the Third Ohio Volunteers, to accompany our transports, (eight in number,) via Smithland and Paducah to Fort Henry, on the Tennessee river, where our command was to re-embark.

A Yankee in Rebel Prisons

We remained at Palmyra one day and a half, during which time every member of the command was actively employed - those to whom the animals were issued that were furnished us at Nashville, "breaking their mules," the remainder scouring the country through in every direction, in quest of animals to put through the same interesting ceremony, during the performance of which the long-eared and stubborn quadruped before mentioned would tax his ingenuity and muscular power to the utmost, to divest himself of his unwelcome rider. And as our' boys were "foot soldiers," they were at first very easily dis-mounted, frequently in a most undignified and unceremonious manner. One witnessing the performance, and not knowing the boys were "breaking mules," would have naturally supposed they belonged to Dan. Rice's, or Van Amburgh's circus, and were a company of trained summer-saulters and tumblers, exercising in their profession for amusement; though could they have been close enough to see the numerous bruised heads and sprained limbs, the illusion would have been soon dispelled. But both of these, or even worse injuries, the boys regarded as of but trivial con-sequence; and now that so *admirable* an opportunity for riding presented itself, they were determined to *ride* at all hazards. It was here that Colonel Streight first discovered the quality of the animals drawn by Quartermaster Doughty, at Nashville. In his report to Major General Thomas, he speaks concerning them as follows:

"The mules issued to me at Nashville were nothing hut poor, wild, unbroken colts, many of them but two years old; a large number of them had the horse distemper; some forty or fifty of the lot were too near dead to travel, and had to be left at the landing, and some ten or twelve died before we started." Those that were able to travel at all were so wild and unmanageable that it took nearly two days to cat.ch and break them; even then a man saddling one was in imminent danger of his life, unless he kept a sharp lookout for the heels of his mule, which were most of the time performing evolutions in the air something after the style of *the wild Highland Fling.*

LEAVE PALMYRA

On the 13th our command left Palmyra and marched about fifteen miles. proceeding by a circuitous route in a south-western direction, camping at night on Yellow Creek, fourteen miles from Fort Donelson. This was our first day's march as mounted infantry, though as yet only about one-third of our' men were mounted; but these were considered by the boy's a most formidable body of cavalry: and they no doubt imagined themselves, mounted on their suddenly metamorphosed war steeds, (mules,) successfully charging and putting to flight massed columns of the enemy's infantry, rushing with yells and fixed bayonets to the conflict.

Nature had donned her most attractive garb, the warm spring sun had already coaxed the early wild flowers to peep modestly forth and adorn fields and woods with their bright hues, which seemed to inspire every soldier with hope and courage, the thought of being prisoner's in the hands of a merciless and inhuman enemy within a month, or ever for that matter, never once entering their minds; but the fortunes of war are of all things the most variable.

PRESSING HORSES AND MULES

Early the next morning we resumed our march, and arrived at Fort Henry about noon on the 15th; we had scoured the country as far south as it was safe, on the account of the proximity of a large force of the enemy in that direction under Woodward.

It will be remembered that we left Nashville with less than eight hundred animals, not quite half enough to mount our command, and many of these entirely useless for the kind of service required. And although about one hundred of our mules gave out and had to be left behind on our march, yet when we reached Fort Henry our animals numbered about twelve hundred; those we had collected in the country were mostly in good condition, but were nearly all barefooted.

It may be asked why we were not furnished with a sufficient number of good animals before leaving Nashville. For the very good reason, that the grand object of the expedition was to cripple the enemy as much as possible; and one very effectual way of doing this, was to seize the animals whose labor furnished subsistence for the rebel armies and roving bands of guerillas, whose dastardly and fiendish deeds have cursed the fairest portions of Kentucky, Tennessee, and other border States. General Rosecrans therefore gave orders to Colonel Streight to mount his command in the above manner; and which could very easily have been done, had there been one-third as much stock in the country as we expected to find; and had there been one-tenth the number General Morgan found in the course of his expedition through Indiana and Ohio, we could have marched to the coast of Florida and back in safety, but on the contrary the line of our expedition afforded but a very few animals, and those of an inferior quality.

Contrary to our expectations, our transports had not yet arrived at Fort Henry, and did not reach there until the evening of the 16th, having been delayed at Paducah, Kentucky, taking on rations and forage for General Dodge's army at Corinth, Mississippi. The whole of that night officers and men were actively engaged embarking the animals, and in other preparations for our departure from Fort Henry. And on the morning of the 17th, when the sun came out bright and beautiful from behind the hills bordering the waters of the Tennessee, his beams mingled with the spray dashed in air by the bows of our vessels as they ploughed impetuously against the current of the grand old river. After a voyage of three days, made delightful and pleasant by the genial smiles of a Southern spring, that gave a garb of beauty and grandeur to the towering hills on either side, and a border of green shrubbery and many colored flowers to the meandering Tennessee, we arrived at Eastport, Mississippi, at that time, in con-sequence of low water, the head of navigation on this river.

LAND AT EASTPORT

Eastport is a steamboat landing in the. north-east corner of the State of Mississippi, and eight miles from Iuka, formerly the scene of one of our gallant Rosey's triumphs. At this time General Dodge, with his Corinth army, was in camp on the banks of Little Bear Creek, ten miles distant, awaiting the arrival of our command, he having received orders to make a demonstration up the Tennessee river, threatening Tuscumbia, Florence, and other points in the valley, for the purpose of covering the movements of our expedition. Soon as our command had disembarked, and directions had been given for camping the brigade and caring for the animals, Colonel Streight started for General Dodge's camp, an interview with that officer being necessary to our future movements.

DISASTROUS AFFAIR

In justice to all parties concerned, it would be well to mention here a circumstance which contributed much, no doubt, to the failure of the expedition. While disembarking and picketing our animals, a stampede was created among them, when nearly three hundred of the best we had escaped. When Colonel Streight returned from General Dodge's camp, he dispatched large scouting parties in every direction in quest of the strayed horses and mules, but only a small portion of the number escaped were recovered; the remainder fell into the hands of the enemy.

The loss of these animals was a heavy blow to the command; for besides detaining us nearly two days at Eastport, and running down our stock in searching the country to recover them, it caused a still further delay at Tuscumbia, to supply their places. Another lot of the mules drawn at Nashville had to be left here, on account of the distemper before mentioned.

ARRIVAL AT AND DEPARTURE FROM TUSCUMBIA

We left Eastport on . the afternoon of the 21st of April, and reached General Dodge's headquarters the following morning at 8 o'clock. We then proceeded in rear of General Dodge's forces, who were continually skirmishing with the enemy, as they advanced, as far as Tuscumbia, Alabama, scouring the country to the river on the left, and to the mountains on our right, and collected in all the horses and mules that could be found.

We arrived at Tuscumbia about five o'clock P. M., on the twenty-fourth day of April. Here General Dodge furnished us with about two hundred mules and six wagons, the latter to haul our ammunition and rations. We now had all but about one hundred and fifty of our men mounted, though some of them very indifferently.

At one o'clock, on the morning of the twenty-sixth, our brigade moved quietly out of camp at this place, taking a south-east course, in the direction of Rome, Georgia. General Dodge, at the same time, advanced with his forces on Courtland, to engage the enemy until we should be beyond pursuit. Had he followed this programme, which was in fact the object of his movement from Corinth - as Colonel Streight expected, and as he assured the Colonel he would do - nothing could have interfered to prevent the expedition being entirely successful in every particular.

The first night after leaving Tuscumbia, our advance, consisting of all our mounted force, camped in the vicinity of Mount Hope, a village in Lawrence county, Alabama, having made a march of thirty-four miles, over mountainous and almost impassable roads. Col. Streight took up his quarters at the house of one of the most wealthy and influential citizens of the place, and withal an arrant traitor; though his daughter, a highly educated and accomplished young lady, professed to sympathise with us and our cause, and did everything in her power for our comfort. In fact, her actions went so far to prove her profess-ions of loyalty, that Colonel S. ordered the Quartermaster to pay her for a beautiful riding pony taken by one of our tired and sore-footed "boys" - it being General Rosecrans' orders to pay all loyal citizens for whatever property taken for the benefit of the command.

The following evening we entered the village of Moulton, the county seat. of Lawrence county, Alabama. Our advance, consisting of Captain Smith's two companies of cavalry, charged into the town about sunset, putting to flight and capturing part of a company of Colonel Roddy's command.

LOYAL CITIZENS

In the county jail, at the above place, had been confined for longer or shorter periods, and at different times, those citizens of the county who, amid the stirring and exciting scenes of a gigantic civil war, and surrounded by armed traitors, still defended the old flag, and battled manfully for the glorious principles of constitutional liberty. Many of these patriotic but persecuted men were, previous to the war, friends and neighbors of the soldiers of Captain Smith's command, who were themselves refugees from their homes and families, having nearly a year previous broken the thousand ties that bound them to their homes and fire-sides, their wives and little ones, to battle even unto death for the holy cause of liberty and human freedom. It was, therefore, with difficulty they were prevented from razing to the ground the building within whose hated walls and filthy cells their friends and relations had been con-fined for weeks and months, and for no other reason than that they remained loyal to the Union, and maintained against all opposition an undying love for the glorious principles upon which the liberties of our country are founded.

We remained at this place only long enough for the men to prepare some slight refreshment for themselves and feed their animals; this was soon accomplished, and before midnight the soldiers of the Provisional Brigade were again in the saddle and on the march.

On the following day we captured a number of wagons, containing a large quantity of bacon, guns ammunition, &c. Such of these prizes as were necessary for the complete equipment of our command, were issued to the men, and the balance destroyed. We also picked up during the day's march a number of animals, which were indeed very much needed, as those drawn at Nashville were failing very fast from excessive fatigue; also from the distemper, before referred to. In fact, from ten o'clock in the morning our line of march was literally strewn with exhausted horses and mules, many of them dead and dying, and it was only by extraordinary labor and exertion that their places were supplied as fast as they gave out.

This day's march brought us to the base of a range of hills, known as the Sand Mountains. Here it was determined to bivouac for the night. The prospect of a few hours rest and sleep, a luxury that had not been enjoyed by any of us for some time previous, gave to our weary men a feeling of happiness that can only be realized by those who have experienced the utter exhaustion of excessive fatigue and long wakefulness. Up to this time we had made slow progress in the direction of the grand object of the expedition, merely marching in that course with our foot soldiers, while our mounted force was engaged, day and night, scouring the country in every direction in search of horses and mules; and now that a sufficient number had been obtained, we were ready to push forward on the following morning with dispatch and rapidity.

BATTLE OF DAY'S GAP

On the morning of April thirtieth, 1863, the sun shone out bright and beautiful, as spring day's sun ever beamed; and from the smouldering camp fires of the previous night the mild blue smoke ascended in graceful curves, and mingled with the gray mist slumbering on the mountain tops above. The scene was well calculated to inspire and refresh the minds of our weary soldiers. But alas! many of the brave souls that spurred their steeds on that beautiful morning, when the command *"Column forward'* was given, were never to see the dawn of another day. Scarcely was the column in motion when our rear was attacked by the enemy's advance; sharp skirmishing continued for some time between our rear guard and one of General Roddy's regiments.

It was Colonel Streight's intention to avoid, if possible, a general engagement, as the prosecution of our expedition towards its intended destination was of vastly more importance than a victory in this locality could possibly be to our cause. But the enemy pressing us closely, and bringing up his artillery, throwing shot and shell into our column, a battle was the only alternative; we therefore, soon as a favorable position was obtained, halted and dismounted, and after concealing our animals in a deep ravine in our rear, formed in line of battle for the coming conflict. It was a novel and imposing sight to witness here amid the blue and towering mountains, covered with the verdure of spring, the green sward smiling a welcome to the season of flowers, and the bright sun, unclouded, lending a genial, refreshing warmth, that little band, with shining bayonets, equipped for the stern conflict of war. The hour for action has come, and the battle of Day's Gap soon commences.

The rebel regiments can be discovered moving into line; the "stars and bars" can be distinctly seen, but opposite floats proudly and defiantly the old stars and stripes - battle flag of the Union and banner of liberty! The Fifty-First and Seventy-Third Indiana Regiments meet and repulse two desperate charges of the enemy. The Third Ohio and Eightieth Illinois have also become engaged. The cannonading is heavy, and the rattle of musketry is sharp, especially on our left. The enemy fights well, for they are principally General Forrest's trained veterans. A loud and prolonged shout now bursts on the ear. It comes from the Third Ohio and Eightieth Illinois, who have charged and taken the enemy's battery. The enemy feel the loss of their guns and their line wavers! Cheer after cheer bursts from our brave boys, for the enemy are giving way! They' are al-ready running in the utmost disorder and confusion. Our gallant soldiers still pursue, making the ground quake and the rebels tremble. The rout is complete and the field is ours. But the victory is won by the sacrifice of some of the best and bravest blood in our heroic little brigade.

Those are proud moments for the soldier, when he stands victorious on the bloody field, and sees the columns of the enemy in full retreat before him.

In this fight the enemy received such a severe chastisement that he would not have dared to pursue us further, had he not been reinforced by a large brigade of Forrest's troops, which, unfortunately for us, came to their assistance while his routed and demoralized masses were fleeing from the scene of their late inglorious defeat. The rebel loss in this engagement was about one hundred and eighty officers and men killed and wounded, including Captain Forrest, a brother of the General. We also took a number of prisoners, about thirty. Our own loss in killed and wounded, was thirty-one officers and men, including the brave and lamented Lieutenant Colonel Sheets, of the Fifty-first Indiana, who fell mortally wounded while leading his regiment in a charge.

REBEL BARBARITIES

We remained on the field of our victory for some time, anticipating a second attack from the enemy, who, now that he was greatly strengthened by the addition of a fresh brigade, no doubt felt confident of making us an easy prey; he did not, however, advance during our occupation of this position.

The best arrangements possible were made for our wounded, whom we were compelled to leave here in a field hospital, leaving with them, however, one of our surgeons, (Dr. Spencer, of the Seventy-Third Indiana,) also such articles for their comfort and sustenance as we had at our disposal. It was with feelings of the deepest regret that we left here in a hostile country, soon to fall into the hands of a merciless foe, our brave and wounded comrades. But the necessities of war are imperative; consequently when the command *forward* was given, we were

A Yankee in Rebel Prisons

compelled to bid adieu, and leave here in the dark mountain ravine, in which our hospital was located, the brave but unfortunate men who had fallen by our sides ill the late severe conflict. The treatment experienced by these men after the enemy advanced and made them their prisoners, was inhuman beyond expression. Every ounce of the bread, meat, sugar, coffee, &c., left for their subsistence, was immediately taken possession of by Forrest and Roddy's unfeeling troopers. And their blankets, and such articles of clothing as had necessarily been taken off, for the moment, were at once converted to the use of these semi-barbarous soldiers. In fact, as these acts of villainy occurred in presence of the rebel officers, we can but infer that it was in accordance with established rules and regulations for these villains on all occasions to exercise their thieving propensities to their complete gratification. It was no unfrequent occurrence for one of them to approach our wounded and helpless officers and men, and rudely take their hats from their heads, perhaps inquire the cost of it, and receiving a proper reply, impudently remark that it was "mighty cheap," and then put it on his own head and walk off. Sometimes, perhaps, they would leave with their helpless and defenceless victims, an old, gray and slouched head covering, that might once have been called a hat, and call it an "even swap." Such scenes as this were common, and only terminated when our men had been robbed of everything valuable about them, including even pocket knives, combs, and other small though useful articles. Even the medicines and surgical instruments, left with Dr. Spencer for the benefit of the wounded, were taken by the rebel surgeons and carried oft'; consequently our men had to lay with their undressed wounds, and suffer the most horrible agony, until death put an end to their misery several of them dying, who, with a little kind treatment and attention, would soon have recovered.

The loyal citizens in the vicinity would have gladly cared for, and given all the comfort and relief in their power to our wounded men, had they been permitted to do so; but the brutal guard would not allow their suffering fellow beings to receive from this source even a cup of milk or piece of bread. But thanks to the kind sympathizing heart and ingenious tact of woman, the vigilance of the rebel soldier was occasionally evaded, and our men were the thankful recipients of some kind favor, or dainty article of diet, smuggled to them and bestowed by her fair hands. Nor were those wounded men, now prisoners of war, the only victims of rebel persecution. The citizens of the surrounding country, who were suspected of loyalty to the Union, were compelled to suffer the greatest indignities and most inhuman treatment, Mrs. Penn, a widow lady residing in the vicinity, and who had two sons with us in Captain Smith's company of Alabama cavalry, seemed to be a special object of their fiendish and malignant barbarities; she and her daugh-ters were driven from their home, her house sacked from cellar to garret, and every article of property she possessed, including female wearing apparel, ruthlessly destroyed, her outhouses and fences burned, and horses and mules turned in on her growing crops.

BATTLE OF CROOKED CREEK

After leaving Day's Gap, we proceeded several miles without any evidence of the, enemy being in pursuit, but about four o'clock in the evening our rear was again attacked, and as we did not want to lose time by halting to give battle, if it could possibly be avoided, the column was kept in motion, skirmishing fighting going on, however, all the time be-tween Captain Smith's two companies of cavalry and the enemy's advance. Captain Smith, with his little handful of men, kept the enemy at bay for more than two hours. .But they were now pressing us so closely that Colonel Streight resolved to halt his command, and again give them battle. In a short time the bloody strife was raging with all the fury of brave und determined men. Charge after charge, made by the enemy, was met and repulsed by our brave boys, who drove back with terrible destruction each successive effort, to dislodge them from the admirable position selected for our line of defense.,

  This engagement raged with greater desperation for some time than the preceding action in the morning. The report of fire-arms was terrific; the flashes from musketry and artillery lighting up the hills on all sides, rendering the scene, although of death and carnage, one of the grandest sublimity. It was now about ten o'clock, yet by the light of the full moon, which looked calmly down on the bloody scene, we were able to discover that the enemy had began to waver and fall back, unable to contend longer against the terrible fire our men were pouring with fearful destruction into their ranks. In a short time all was quiet, and the still air of night, that .but a few moments before resounded with the roar of artillery and musketry, was only broken by the lonely notes of the whip-poor-will, as they came from his secluded spot in the surround-ing forest. And the Provisional Brigade was victorious on two bloody fields in one day. But we lost in killed and wounded some brave and valuable men; among the number who fell in this engagement, was the brave and gallant young adjutant of the Eightieth Illinois, Lieutenant J. C. Jones.

The enemy in this action had their whole force engaged, yet, by the skillful maneuvering of our little brigade, we met and repulsed them at every point. To this, and the bravery and determination of our men, we alone can ascribe our success in meeting and driving back discomfitted numbers, so much our superior, and having at their command several heavy field pieces. Our artillery consisted only of two small mountain howitzers, and the two pieces taken from Forrest in the morning; for the latter we had but a small quantity of ammunition, the caisons being nearly empty when captured; they were, therefore, soon of no service, and were ordered by the Colonel to be spiked, and the carriages cut down.

CAPTURE OF DR. KING

From the earliest moments of the above bloody scene, Dr. Peck, Medical Director, and his assistants, were active in collecting and caring for our wounded; but before this arduous, yet humane duty·, was accomplished, our command , was in motion - in fact had advanced some considerable distance - and a rebel regiment had already formed and started in pursuit; consequently to rejoin the brigade, Drs. Peck and King, who, regardless of personal safety, still remained with our wounded, had to pass along the full length of this regiment, which they did with safety and without creating any suspicion; but after passing the head of the column, it occurred to the " rebs" that they were "real live Yankees," and the foremost of the party shouted several times at the top of his voice for them to halt, and started with a half dozen comrades in pursuit, the whole party discharging their carbines after the flying disciples of AEsculapius fortunately without effect, though being well mounted they soon overtook Dr. King, whom they made a prisoner. Dr. Peck, mounted on his favorite little roan, was by this time considerably advanced, consequently was able to escape, and soon rejoined the command.

AMBUSHING THE ENEMY

Colonel Streight, anticipating an advance of Forrest's forces, soon as it was known to them that we were moving, directed Colonel Hathaway, with his regiment, (Seventy-Third Indiana,) to lay concealed in the heavy timber nearby, for the purpose of ambushing them in case of an immediate advance. But a few moments elapsed before the enemy's column was discovered approaching; and soon their advance battalion came up unsuspectingly within forty yards of our concealed regiment, which at that instant poured a full volley of musketry into their ranks, sending them back, pell mell, in the greatest consternation and disorder, with the full conviction, no doubt, that every tree for miles around concealed a Yankee soldier with a musket charged to the muzzle. But relying on the advantage of being in their own country, consequently acquainted with every road and by-path, also conscious of their superior numbers, they soon rallied, and attacked us again about two o'clock in the morning, when Colonel Streight again resolved to ambush them; which proved so successful, and gave them such a taste of Yankee courage and skill, that we had no further annoyance until about eleven o'clock next day, when our pickets were attacked just as we were leaving Blountsville, where we had halted to feed our animals and refresh the exhausted and fatigued men, who had not had a moments rest for two days and nights.

CHAPTER II.

BURNING BLACK CREEK BRIDGE

On the morning of May 2nd we crossed Black Creek, near Gadsden, Alabama, on a fine wooden bridge, which was afterwards burned by our rear guard. This, it was thought, would delay Forrest's forces long enough to enable us to reach Rome, Georgia, before he could again overtake us, as the stream was very deep and seemed to be unfordable. But among a lot of prisoners captured by us in the morning, and paroled, was a young man by the name of Sansom, who, soon as set at liberty, made his way direct to the pursuing force of General Forrest, and piloted that officer and his command to a ford where the whole force soon crossed and started again in pursuit of our brigade. From this incident the rebels manufactured the following bit of romance:

"General Forrest had been pursuing the enemy all day, and was close upon their heels, when the pursuit was effectually checked by the destruction by the enemy of a bridge over a deep creek, which, for the time, separated pursuer am} pursued. The country was exceedingly wild and rugged, and the banks of the creek too steep for passage on horseback. General Forrest rode up to a modest little farm house on the road side, and seeing a young maiden standing upon the little stoop in front of the dwelling, he accosted her, and inquired if there was any ford or passage for his men across the creek above or below the destroyed bridge. The young girl proceeded to direct him, with animated gesture, and cheeks flushed with excitement, and almost breathless in her eagerness to aid the noble cause of the gallant Confederate General.

It was a scene for a painter. The Southern girl, her cheeks glowing and her bright eyes flashing, while her mother, attracted by the colloquy; stood holding the door, and gazing upon the cavalcade over her venerable spectacles, the cavalry chieftain resting his legs carelessly over the saddle-pommel, his staff drawn up around him, and his weather-worn veterans scattered in groups about the road, and some of them actually nod-ding in their saddles from excessive fatigue. After some further inquiry, General Forrest asked the young lady if she would not mount behind him and show him the way to the ford. She hesitated, and turned to her mother an inquiring look. The mother, with a delicacy becoming a prudent parent, rather seemed to object to her going with the soldiers. 'Mother,' she said, ' I am not afraid to trust myself with as brave a man as General Forrest.'

'But, my dear, folks will talk about you.'

'Let them talk,' responded the heroic girl, ' I must go.' .And with that she lightly sprang upon the roots of a fallen tree, Forrest drew his mettled charger near her, she grasped the hero fearlessly about the waist and sprung up be-hind him, and away they went - over brake and bramble, through the glade, and on towards the ford. The route was a difficult one, even for as experienced a rider as Forrest., but his fair young companion and guide held her seat like an experienced horsewoman, and without the slightest evidence' of fear. At length they drew near to the ford. Upon the high ridge above, the quick eye of Forrest descried the Yankee sharpshooters, dodging from tree to tree, and pretty soon an angry minie whistled by his ear.

'What was that, General Forrest?' asked the maiden.

'Bullets,' he replied; 'are you afraid?'

She replied in the negative, and they proceeded on. At length it became necessary, from the density of the undergrowth and snags, to dismount, and Forrest hitched his horse, and the .girl preceded him, leading the way herself - remarking that the Yankees would not fire upon her, and they might fire if he went first. To this Forrest objected, not wishing to screen himself behind the brave girl; and, taking the lead himself, the two proceeded on to the ford under the fire of the Yankee rear guard. Having discovered the route he returned, brought up his axemen and cleared out a road, and safely crossed his whole column.

Upon taking leave of his fair young guide, the General asked if there was anything he might do for her in return for her invaluable services, She told him that the Yankees on ahead had her brother prisoner, and if General Forrest would only release him she should be more than repaid. The General took out his watch, and examined it. It was just five minutes to eleven. 'Tomorrow,' he said, 'at five minutes to eleven o'clock, your brother shall be returned to you.' And so the sequel proved. Streight, with his whole command, was captured at ten the next morning. Young Sansom was released, and dispatched on the fleetest horse in the command to return to his heroic sister, whose courage and presence of mind had

A Yankee in Rebel Prisons

contributed so much to the success of one of the most remarkable cavalry pursuits and captures known in the world's history."

The true version of this story is, as near as possible, as follows: Whenever we captured any prisoners, they were immediately paroled, and not taken along with the command any distance; especially not forty or fifty miles, as this rebel romance would indicate. And the young Confederate soldier, Sansom, was with General Forrest when our command surrendered, not notwithstanding his solemn oath not to aid or comfort in any manner whatever the enemies of the United States, was fully armed and equipped, and boasted that it was the bullet shot from his gun that killed the noble Hathaway.

BATTLE OF BLUNT'S FARM

Soon after crossing Black Creek, we passed through the town of Gadsden, where we destroyed a quantity of rebel stores, and captured some prisoners. We then proceeded on to Blunt's plantation, where we halted for the purpose of giving the men an opportunity of preparing a hasty meal for themselves and to feed their animals. But the anticipated pleasure of a cup of steaming coffee, which the Union soldier considers one of his indispensables, was soon dispelled by the report of musketry in the direction of our picket line. The command was immediately given to prepare for action and almost instantly every man ill the Provisional Brigade seized his gun, and was marching out bravely and defiantly to engage once more the vastly superior force of the enemy, with whom we had contended successfully for three days, and had completely routed and defeated in two regular pitched battles.

Colonel Hathaway, with his regiment, was directed to the front and center, to support our two howitzers, which were doing such fearful execution in the ranks of the enemy, that they seemed to have resolved to capture them if possible, regardless of the cost in blood. Their efforts, however, were fruitless, for although nearly every gunner and man connected with the two pieces was either killed or wounded, Colonel Hathaway so determinedly maintained his position that the enemy recoiled in the greatest confusion, our men pouring a perfect hail of lead into his retreating columns. This action lasted for nearly three hours, the enemy charging our lines from right to left repeatedly, but was as often repulsed, with severe loss, by our gallant regiments. When the sun set on that tranquil evening, sinking slowly down behind the forest, unstirred by the least breath of wind, the sharp and bloody struggle was decided. The enemy was retreating badly hurt; his dead men and horses strewing their line of retreat.

Our heroes won the day by hard and desperate fighting, but lost in the struggle one of the most valiant hearts that ever beat. He was in the performance of his duty, riding along his skirmish line, waving his hat and cheering his men on, when he received a pulmonary wound from a minie ball, cutting a large blood vessel, from which he died almost instantly. And the noble, the chivalric, the gallant Hathaway, was no more. He fell, the noblest of sacrifices on the altar of his country, to whose glorious service he had dedicated his life. Thus passed away a noble, lofty soul; thus ended a career full of arduous, glorious, and splendid achievements. He was ever with that part of his regiment which was under the hottest fire, and when the enemy shifted their fire to other portions, he proceeded thither and directed the movements of each company in person. His men will remember how cheering and inspiring was his presence with them – how his cool-ness steadied them in the most exciting moments - and his brave, cheerful voice, was the herald of success. His character was so frank, and open, and beautiful-his bearing so modest and full of simplicity, that he conciliated all hearts, and made every one who met him his friend.

Thus modest, brave, loving and beloved -;the famous soldier, the charming companion, he was called away from the scenes of his triumphs and glory, to a brighter world, where neither war nor rumors of war ever come, and wounds, and pain, and suffering are unknown; where…

"Malice domestic, foreign levy, nothing can touch him further!"

PROSPECTS OF SUCCESS

Affairs were now rapidly approaching a crisis; every one felt that the next twenty-four hours would decide the fate of our expedition. We were now within sixty miles of Rome, the point at which we designed crossing the Coosa river; and if we could reach that place before a force could be thrown in to check our further advance, complete success would be inevitable; for once on the opposite side of the river, and the bridge destroyed after us, the pursuit of Forrest would be effectually checked, and we would then have ample time to recruit the exhausted energies of our men and animals; besides, if necessary we could soon obtain an entire fresh supply of the latter; and could then either fight or decline battle at our own option. On the contrary, should there be a force collected at Rome sufficient to prevent us crossing the bridge, there would be no alter-native left us but to surrender, the exhausted condition of our men and animals rendering escape by any route, strategy, or valor in battle, an impossibility. To guard against the above contingency, Captain Russell, of the Fifty-First Indiana, was ordered with two hundred picked men, mounted on our best horses, to proceed with the greatest dispatch to Rome and take possession of the river bridge, railroad stock, and telegraph lines, before the forces there could make preparation for defence, or troops be brought from Atlanta and other points on the railroad, in case they were advised by couriers from General Forrest, or otherwise, of the advance of our expedition.

After some active demonstrations, and stragetic movements, designed to impress the enemy with the belief that we were preparing for a renewal of the contest at the earliest dawn of day, the balance of the command moved on as fast as the fatigued condition of our animals would permit.

LOSE OUR ROUTE

Strong hopes were now entertained of success and would, no doubt, have been realized, had not our guide misled us in regard to the ford by which to cross the Chattoogee river. In justice to him, however, it is but proper to remark, that he was a true and faithful man, and this, the only instance in which he seemed at fault; but this irreparable mistake took us at least twelve miles out of our direct course, be-sides otherwise delaying us.

We marched all this night, making four consecutive days and nights in the saddle, except when fighting or feeding our animals. It was during this, our last night's march, that one of our scouting parties destroyed the Round Mountain Iron Works, situated in the Cherokee Valley, about thirty miles from Rome. These works were, at the time, largely engaged manufacturing ordnance and material for the rebel army, and employed nearly one thousand hands.

CAPTAIN RUSSELL'S PARTY

Our vanguard, consisting of two hundred men, under command of Captain Milton Russell, of the Fifty-First Indiana., arrived in the vicinity of Rome about eight o'clock next morn-ing after the battle of Blunt's Farm, at least four hours later than it was expected they would reach that point, but their animals were so completely exhausted that it had been impossible for them to get there sooner, as they had rode all night at the utmost speed of their jaded horses. By this time the city was full of armed men. General Forrest's courier (a citizen of Gadsden) having arrived six hours previous, gave the first intelligence of our near approach, so rapidly and dexterously had our movements been executed. But, in this short time, a large number of troops had been hurried from Atlanta, Kingston and Dalton; besides, the citizens and home-guards for miles around, had been collected and put under arms, several pieces of artillery had also been put in position commanding the river bridge and every avenue by which the city could be app-roached. The floor of the bridge was torn up and piled with straw and turpentine, ready to ignite, in case an attempt was made to force a crossing. The following extract from the Rome Courier, of the Tuesday morning following, will, I hope, satisfy the incredulous of the nature and extent of the preparations made for our reception.

A Yankee in Rebel Prisons

The Courier says:

"Sunday morning last, opened at half-past two o'clock A. M., with an alarm. Mr. John H. Wisdam, a resident of Gadsden, Alabama, and a former resident of this city, reached here, after riding with hot haste for eleven hours, and gave information that the enemy were at Gadsden when he left, and were bound for Rome. Preparations were begun with dispatch, and by seven o'clock in the morning, our soldiery and citizens were prepared to give them a warm reception. Several pieces of artillery were placed in position commanding the road and river bridge. Cotton barricades were erected at all the defiles near the city, videttes sent out to watch the enemy's approach. Everything was got in readiness for determined resistance. During the morning several couriers arrived with dispatches from General Forrest, urging our commander here to hold them at bay a few hours if possible, and at all hazards.

About half-past eight o'clock A. M., a small body of the enemy's advance (about two hundred) reached the environs of the city; and were actually bold enough to dismount and feed their horses in sight of the city. They picked up all the horses and mules in the neighborhood, took some of our soldiers and citizens prisoners, and reconnoitered the defences of the city."

Among the prisoners referred to in the above extract, was a. rebel mail carrier; he was met on the road by Captain Russell's men when within a few miles of Rome. He at first declined accompanying our " boys" who were going in the direction from whence he just came, but the Captain assured him that the "Yankees" were but a short distance behind, and that if he continued his route, he would undoubtedly fall into their hands. It needed no further argument to induce him to "change front" and proceed with our men in the direction of Rome.

Whether the Captain will consider it a compliment or otherwise, i will state that the rebel "post-boy" supposed he was one of For-rest's Colonels, consequently was very familiar and talkative, and furnished him with much valuable information concerning the numbers and disposition of the troops and defences of the city. It is difficult to imagine his surprise and consternation when our men were attacked by the rebel pickets sent out from Rome - he turned instantly pale as a corpse; and tremblingly gasped that he "guessed the Yankees had already got him." On his arrival in the vicinity of Rome, Captain Russell immediately reconoitered its defences and military strength, which were, indeed, quite formidable, yet notwithstanding the Captain and his gallant "two hundred" would have attempted to enter its limits but for the condition of the river bridge as before stated. The excitement and panic created throughout all this portion of Dixie by our unexpected appearance, was truly diverting. Many of the cowardly traitors, no doubt, really thought that the day of retribution had come.

The "Atlanta Confederacy" of Monday morning, May 4th, says:

"Yesterday (Sunday) morning about three o'clock, Colonel Lee received a dispatch from Major Rawlins, stating that the Yankees were at Gadsden on the Coosa river, and were bound for Rome; he immediately got in readiness, and with his own regiment and all that remained of the provost guards, and some others, took

A Yankee in Rebel Prisons

the train at five o'clock A. M., intending to go to the defense of that place, or any other point where his presence might be needed."

The same paper also contains the following letter from conductor Smith, on the Rome Railroad, to a Mr. Stillwell;

Kingston, May 3d, 1863.

"MR. C. H. Stillwell - Dear Sir: I learned this morning that the Yankees were below Rome, and that our men needed reinforcements. I then ran the train to Rome from this place to carry about seven hundred men, and have just returned, having learned the following particulars: General Forrest has overtaken the enemy at Gaylesville, Cherokee county, Alabama, about twenty miles west of Rome, and the courier stated that an engagement had taken place, The courier left before the fight closed, therefore we can't tell the result. I have a dispatch from General Forrest to General Bragg, asking for a force to be sent to Rome to check them. Their advance came within eight miles of Rome this morning, and drove in our pickets. They numbered two hundred. Their whole force is about fifteen hundred. We have the bridges guarded, and feel confident of our ability to hold them. Mrs. Stillwell is at Oliver's. The bullets flew thick around your house, but your family are all safe. We do not fear any attack between here and Rome. The enemy burnt Noble's Iron Works. We need more men. If Forrest fails to check them, then good by to Rome.

"Yours, Respectfully,

"C. A. SMITH,

"Conductor of the Rome Railroad."

SURRENDER TO GENERAL FORREST

Notwithstanding the chastisement we gave the enemy the previous evening, in the engagement at Blunt's Farm, and the intimidation caused by our subsequent demonstrations, the delay occasioned by our guide's mistake, enabled him to overtake us about nine o'clock next morning, (Sunday, May 3d,) near Gaylesville, Alabama, where we had halted to feed our animals.

They soon attacked us, and after some slight skirmishing, General Forrest sent a flag of truce to Colonel Streight, demanding a surrender. The Colonel held a consultation with the regimental commanders, in which our situation and chances of success were fully canvassed. We had but a small quantity of artillery ammunition, and the few rounds of rifle and musket cartridges on hands, were unfit for service. The enemy had a brigade on our left endeavoring to flank us, and was, in fact, at this time, nearer Rome than we were. Our men were completely exhausted, having had no rest for four days and nights. While General Forrest, having the advantage of good horses, had been able to rest his command, at least half of each night, his soldiers were, therefore, fresh and vigorous compared with the fatigued and worn-out condition of both our men and animals. Captain Russell, with the advance of two hundred men, as has already been shown, was unable to cross the river at Rome. It was evident that we had now to contend with a superior force, both in front and rear. All circumstances taken into consideration, our situation seemed hopeless. It was, therefore, decided to surrender on the following terms: Each regiment to retain its colors, and the officers and men their private property, including the side arms of he former. These terms were agreed to by General Forrest. Our brigade was then drawn up in line, our arms stacked, and we were prisoners of war.

CHAPTER III

ARRIVE AT ROME

The same day that we were made prisoners we were marched under guard to Rome. A considerable change in the programme we had proposed following, in regard to our entry of that place. But I trust the preceding chapters are sufficient evidence that the alteration was no fault of ours.

The citizens of the place gave unmistakable proof of their joy to see us; but had we entered their town as we expected to have done, I very much doubt if the ladies would have thronged the streets with gay dresses, gaudy ribbons, and smiling faces, to greet us. At least I am informed that there was no demonstration of joy, when the Union troops entered the town a year afterwards, as conquerors.

We remained in Rome until Tuesday morning, May 5th, under orders of General Forrest, who, to his credit be it said, furnished us with sufficient rations for our subsistence, also with comfortable quarters. Though here, as in. every other Southern city through which we passed, every insult that a low, malignant, unprincipled and debased spirit could invent, was heaped upon us by the citizens, who crowded around the cars to express their contempt for" Yankees," and to boast of the superiority and nobleness of the chivalric Southerner.

But even then, during the brightest days of rebellion, unmistakable evidence of loyal sentiment was everywhere visible, but so intimidated by Jeff Davis' bayonets, that it dare not openly manifest itself. Though at some points on our route, when unnoticed by the guard, the ladies would present some of our officers with choice bouquets, whose pressed and faded leaves they still retain as tributes of Southern devotion to the Union, and sympathy for those who have battled for the "glorious flag."

ARRIVAL AT LIBBY PRISON

The officers of our command arrived at Richmond and were placed in the Libby Prison on the sixteenth day of May. We were informed by the rebel officials, that we would be detain-ed there a few days, perhaps three or four, awaiting the arrival of a flag of truce boat from Fortress Monroe to convey us North; we were indeed most gloomy. Had we then known that we should have to remain within the gloomy walls of "Libby" for twelve long, tedious and weary mouths, never for once breathing the pure air of heaven, and without a glimpse of bright sunshine or blue sky, except through the grated bars of the narrow windows, it is impossible to conjecture the depressing influence the information would have had upon our spirits. "Tis well indeed for our race that the events of the future are beyond the fathom of human ken.

On the fifth day of our incarceration in Libby, the anxiously looked for boat arrived from Fortress Monroe, at City Point. Our hearts beat joyfully at the prospect of liberty, and of once more enjoying the protecting folds of our much loved flag. But we were doomed to bitter disappointment. Other prisoners, captured after we were, were sent away in return for the rebel prisoners brought up by our Commissioner, and we were informed that we would be exchanged when the next boat arrived. This was some consolation.

A Yankee in Rebel Prisons

Though we were of course justly indignant that we were not sent off on the first boat, as, according to the rules of the cartel, prisoners were always exchanged in the order of their capture.

At the appointed time, another boat arrived from Fortress Monroe, with a sufficient number of prisoners to exchange for our entire command; but our Commissioner was informed by' the rebel authorities that we would not be given up; but that we would be delivered to the Governor of Alabama, to be dealt with according to the laws of that State for inciting servile insurrection, alleging that during our expedition we had armed and pressed negro slaves into the military service of the United States. This was a gross fabrication, with no foundation in truth; in fact the charge was never afterwards officially brought against us.

In consequence of this act of the rebel authorities, all exchanges of prisoners at once ceased. New and intricate questions, including the exchange of negro soldiers, and their white officers, were from time to time brought up for negotiation. The length of time thus consumed is well known; days, weeks and months passed wearily and tediously away, but brought us no relief.

In the meantime the Libby was becoming daily more populous; prisoners were being brought in from every section - reverses seemed to be overtaking our arms in every quarter -rebel cannon were planted in sight of the dome of our National Capitol; the columns of Lee were rapidly penetrating the great State of Pennsylvania; Vicksburg seemed impregnable to all the force that could be brought against it, and defiant of all the skill that military science could devise; Rosecrans appeared to be un-able to move his army, Bragg still maintaining a strong position in his front, occupying nearly as much of the territory of Tennessee as before the hard fought battle of Murfreesboro. General Morgan had crossed the Ohio river with a large cavalry force, and was spreading devastation and ruin through the States of Indiana and Ohio, marching his column almost in sight of our great Western Metropolis, the beautiful city of Cincinnati. Rebellion, for the time, seemed to triumph over every obstacle. Thus to the de-privations, inhuman treatment, and indignities to which we were subjected, as prisoners of a semi-barbarous foe, was added torturing anxiety for the fate of our country: and the honor of the old flag, whose folds we had flung to the breeze on many bloody fields.

But, thank God! the dark clouds then lowering over our entire country, ready to burst forth in their terrible fury, and destroy at once the noble fabric of Constitutional liberty, only aroused the patriot hearts of our country's sons to a full realization of the dangers of the approaching storm; and the heights of Gettysburg attest how well and nobly they met its first and most terrific outbreak.

Since then the sun of freedom, like the orb of day after a summer's shower, has shone brighter and clearer. Victory has crowned our arms on almost every field. And now, not an armed body of rebels can be found in any State of the Union. Nor does a single Union soldier longer remain in the rebel prisons of the South.

LIBBY PRISON

Libby Prison, the noted bastille of the short-lived military despotism of Jeff Davis, is situated on the south-east corner of

A Yankee in Rebel Prisons

Carey and Eighteenth streets. It stands within a few yards of the Lynchburg canal, and in full view of the rapid waters of the James. The building is three stories high, one hundred and sixty-five feet front, and one hundred and five feet deep. The ground floor is separated into several apartments, in one of which is the prisoners' hospital; the others are used by the rebel Commissary Department, and as offices for the officials connected with the prison. The second and third floors were each divided into three rooms, one hundred and five feet long by forty-five feet wide. At each end of these rooms are five windows, grated with substantial wrought iron bars, one inch and a half in diameter. These, although they answered very well to keep us in, did not keep out the chilling blast of winter.

In the narrow limits of these six rooms were confined for many months nearly eleven hundred United States officers, prisoners of war. This included all our room for cooking, eating, washing, bathing and sleeping.

UNION LADIES INSULTED

The 23rd day of June the officers of General Milroy's command, captured at Winchester, arrived at Libby. The wives of a number of these officers were with their husbands at the above place at the time of their capture. The ladies desired to go home, and begged permission of the rebel authorities to do so, but the privilege was not granted and they were ruthlessly dragged by the rebel soldiery, by order of General Ewell, to the city of Richmond, and cast into a filthy military prison, where they were the victims of the grossest insults and abuses from the rebel officials having them in charge.

The Richmond Examiner, a paper that howled louder than any other in the South, in condemnation of General Butler's order in regard to the women of New Orleans, the next morning after their arrival at Richmond, contained the following article:

"A PRECIOUS GANG. - There arrived on yesterday a gang of depraved women from Winchester, where they had been established by Milroy and his command, to render more complete the unlicensed character of the military government they had established in that unfortunate place. They numbered eighteen in all. They have been furnished with appropriate quarters in the Eastern District Military Prison."

Chivalric editor, while perusing these lines did no blush of shame tingle your cheek? Did no thought arise in your mind of a wife, mother or sister, that might some time be unprotected, and subject to the insults of some dastardly villain of your own stamp? Noble editor! *you* should indeed boast of the "high-toned, courteous, chivalrous and gallant gentlemen of the South."

FOURTH OF JULY IN LIBBY

For some days previous to the anniversary of our National Independence, the prisoners confined in Libby were actively engaged in preparations for a grand celebration on that day. Although we might celebrate St. Patrick's day or Christmas without a flag, we could not think of a jubilee on the Fourth of July without the stars and stripes. But how to get them seemed to be a question which no one could solve. At length a meeting was called to take the matter into consideration. The patriotic and zealous promptly assembled, suggestions and plans were advanced and canvassed, but all seemed impracticable. At length a Connecticut officer of a. fertile brain, observing that some of the prisoners wore red flannel, and others what had once been white cotton, or linen, proposed that each officer contribute a stripe from the lower extremity of his shirt. An ensign of the navy was also required to furnish from the same garment a square for the blue field. The proposition was acceded to with shouts and cheers. Those that were not called on to contribute material were selected as the manufacturers. By the fourth we had a respectable looking flag, and were prouder of it than if it had been made anywhere else, or under any other circumstances, of the finest silk. But alas! poor flag, like your creators, you were doomed to be captured!

Our celebration exercises commenced. Our flag, which until now had been closely concealed from the eyes of rebel officials, was brought to light, and amid cheers and loud huzzas, suspended from one of the beams in the "Upper West Room." The proper officers were nominated. Lieutenant Colonel Irvine made a few patriotic remarks, appropriate for the occasion. Col. Streight then took the stand beneath our flag, and was proceeding to address us, when we were interrupted by the appearance of one of the prison officials, inquiring what we were at. His eye soon caught sight of our stars and stripes; he at once divined the object of the assemblage, and rudely ordered us to take that "hateful rag" down, informing us at the same time that Fourth of July celebrations were not tolerated in the land of "Dixie." No one seemed inclined to obey his order in regard to taking down the flag, and he was permitted to perform the gallant act himself. .

Major T. P. Turner considered it quite a. trophy, and was anxious to know how we got it in prison. He afterwards informed one of our officers that he was going to present it to one of his lady friends, as a relic of the war, and would like to have its full history.

Thus ended our Fourth of July celebration in Libby. From which it will be seen that Southern people are so thoroughly imbued with hatred for the Government of the United States, and everything pertaining thereto, that they sacrilegiously curse the day held sacred by every American citizen.

CHAPTER IV

INCREASING BARBARITIES

As the number of prisoners increased in Libby, our rations decreased in quantity and deteriorated in quality, until the amount furnished us by the rebel commissariat was not actually sufficient to sustain life and health

The continued and increasing indignities to which we were subjected, the insufficient amount of food furnished us, and the general inhuman treatment we received at the hands of those having us in charge, were acts so inhuman and unparalleled in the history of civilized warfare, that it was thought impossible that our condition was known to those chief in authority. Colonel Streight, therefore, on behalf of himself and fellow prisoners, addressed the following most bold and scathing letter to the rebel Secretary of War, demanding of that functionary, for himself and fellow prisoners, such treatment as the usages of civilized warfare accords to prisoners of war:

LIBBY PRISON, RICHMOND, VA.
August 31st, 1863.

HON. JAMES A. SEDDON,
Secretary of War:

Sir - I take the liberty of addressing you on behalf of myself and fellow prisoners, in relation to our situation.

About six hundred of as are confined here, with an average space of about twenty-eight square feet each, which includes our room for cooking, eating, washing, bathing, and sleeping. Our rations consist, as nearly as I can judge as to quantity, of about one-fourth pound of *poor* fresh beef, one-half pound of bread, and one-half gill of rice or black peas, for each man per day. This amount has been found insufficient to sustain life and health in our close prison confinement.

Scorbutic diseases have already appeared, proving fatal in one instance, (Major Morris,) and impairing seriously, if not permanently, the health of many others.

Our sanitary condition would have been much worse than it now is, but for the large purchases of vegetables and other provisions, amounting to nearly one thousand dollars per day, which we have been allowed to make. But as nearly all our money was taken from us when we entered the prison, the daily expenditure of this large sum has at length about exhausted what was left us. We have also been notified that we would not be allowed to receive any portion of the money taken from us here, nor to receive such sums as have been sent to us from home since our imprisonment; though before writing for these monies, we were expressly assured by your officers having us in charge that we would be allowed to receive them.

It will be perceived from the above statement, that our immediate prospective condition is, to say the least, that of semi-starvation. The rations furnished by your Government, may be as good, and as much as it can afford under the circumstances, but in that case it does seem that we should be allowed to purchase the necessary amount to sustain us. It can not possibly be that it is intended to reduce to a famishing condition six hundred prisoners of war. Humanity can not contemplate such a thing without feelings of the deepest horror. Saying nothing of our rights as prisoners of war, even criminals, guilty of the blackest crimes, are not, among civilized people, confined for any length of time on insufficient food.

I wish further to state to you, that previous to my surrender, I made a stipulation with General Forrest, to whom I surrendered, that all private property, including money, belonging to my officers and men, should be respected. This stipulation, in the handwriting of General Forrest, over his own signature, is now in the hands of General Winder, having been taken from me here. Notwithstanding this, my officers (ninety-five in number) have been notified with the balance, that their money has been turned over to Confederate authorities.

For the purpose of avoiding further loss of money, or misunderstanding, and if possible to obtain relief from the unhappy situation in which we are placed, you are most respectfully requested to state in your answer to this communication, the manner in which we will be allowed to obtain the necessary food and clothing to render us comfortable.

I have the honor to be, Sir,

Your most obedient servant,

A. D. STREIGHT,

Colonel of Fifty-First Indiana Volunteers

PERFIDY OF UNION OFFICERS

The above secured to us, for a short time, an increased amount of rations, and mitigated, in a great degree, the barbarous treatment and indignities to which we had hitherto been subject.

Among the six hundred Union officers confined at this time in Libby, there were a few who seemed to be in the wrong army. They were, at all times, and in every conceivable manner, courting the favor of the rebel authorities, and allowed their evil passions to carry them so far that they got up a counter statement to the above communication of Colonel Streight's for which they were granted many privileges and favors not enjoyed by the other prisoners of war.

In their statements of the rations furnished, they make out a bill of fare nearly as varied as would be found at a first-class hotel. They succeeded in inducing the two officers acting as commissaries for their fellow-prisoners, to make these vouchers of kind treatment and bounteous fare; therefore, under the circumstances which it was done, they received no part of the condemnation attached to the names of the two officers of high rank who drew up and indorsed the statements, consequently their names are not given in connection with the communications which appear below:

LIBBY PRISON, FIRST OFFICERS' QUARTERS,
April 18th, 1863.

CAPTAIN: Having learned that a communication has been sent to the Secretary of War by Colonel Streight, of the Fifty-First Indiana Volunteers, U. S. A., complaining of the quantity of food furnished to the occupants of this floor of the Libby Prison, I wish to make the following statement, in pure justice to you and your commissary W. Burnham, whose efforts in our behalf deserves our gratitude and thanks, also to relieve any impressions on your mind that I or the mass of my fellow-prisoners participate in the feeling of dissatisfaction and complaint evinced in the communication above referred to - Colonel Streight being resident on this floor. For the last three days I have witnessed the weighing of 159 pounds of beef and 236 pounds of bread each day; also rations of vinegar, soap, rice or beans. Our number is two hundred and ninety-nine, making the ration of beef one-half pound, and bread one pound and two ounces to each man. In my knowledge, about the same quantity and quality of food has been dispensed to us for the last two months. In conclusion, permit me to bear testimony of the kind and courteous treatment that we have received at the hands of the officers connected with the prison.

[Signed] ********

To CAPTAIN J. WARNER,
A. Q. M. C. S. Military Prison.

LIBBY PRISON, SECOND OFFICERS' QUARTERS,
September 18th, 1863.

CAPTAIN: At the request of your urbane and attentive commissary W. Burnham, I cheerfully make the following statement: The number of prisoners occupying this floor, is two hundred and fifty-four; there has been issued to us 127 pounds of beef and 285 pounds of bread, which has all been weighed in my presence, being an allowance of one-half pound beef and one pound and two ounces of bread to each man; also rations of vinegar, candles, soap, salt, rice and beans. These articles are of good quality, and to the best of my belief about the same quantity and quality as we have been receiving for the last two months. I will also here state, that my knowledge of the feelings of my fellow-prisoners, warrants me in saying that a general sentiment of satisfaction is entertained towards all the officers connected with the prison.

[Signed] *******

CAPTAIN J. WARNER
A. Q. M. C. S. Military Prison.

Accompanying the above certificate was the following indorsement:

LIBBY PRISON, RICHMOND, VA
September 18th, 1863.

We fully indorse the within, trusting it may correct a statement which is false and unjust, emanating from one of the inmates of this prison. But, in doing so, we wish only to speak for ourselves individually, without referring to the sentiments of any other officer.

[Signed]

JAMES M. SANDERSON,
Lt. Col. and Com. Sub. of First Corps.

CHAS. W. TILDEN,
Colonel of Sixteenth Maine Volunteers

INDIGNATION OF THE PRISONERS

This flunkeyism and usurpation, of authority on the part of these officers, created in all the other prisoners confined in Libby, a feeling of the greatest indignity. For the rations furnished us were of no better quality, nor more in quantity, than set forth in the communication of Colonel Streight. Moreover, it was a notorious fact, that all of these officers daily made large purchases of fresh meats and vegetables - a strange phenomenon - when the rebel commissariat furnished them with such an extensive and varied bill of fare.

A meeting of the prisoners was called to express their sentiments in regard to these false and malignant statements. The following resolutions were offered and unanimously adopted:

Resolved 1. That the written statement addressed to Captain J. Warner, Commissary of Subsistence of C. S. A., indorsed and vouched for by Colonel Charles W. Tilden, Sixteenth Maine Volunteers, and Lieutenant Colonel James M. Sanderson, Commissary of Subsistence of First Army Corps U. S. .A., in reference to the treatment and sentiments of the officer confined here, is, in every essential particular, a gross misrepresentation of facts, and in its reasonable inferences unqualifiedly false.

Resolved 2. That said statement is directly calculated to stifle the voice of our reasonable complaints as truthfully set forth in the communication of Colonel A. D. Streight, which they stigmatize as unjust and untrue, to mislead and deceive our commissioner for exchange of prisoners, and our Government.

Resolved 3. That in lieu of the cruel and inhuman treatment of the enlisted men of our army by the Confederate authorities, which daily comes under our notice, not to speak of the indignities and deprivations to which our officers have been subjected, the action of those officers, whose names are attached to the communication referred to in the first, meets our unqualified condemnation.

Resolved 4. That our thanks are due to Colonel Streight for his fearless and unselfish efforts to secure for us additional accommodations from our enemies; and that an increased amount of rations are some of the fruits of his labors; and that the course he has pursued, in relation to our condition, meets with our hearty approval hearty approval.

STARVED TO DEATH

During the first months of our confinement in Libby, one of the rooms below the officers' quarters, was used as a prison for our enlisted men. These poor fellows, even when they had money, were not allowed to purchase anything whatever, but were confined exclusively to rations issued them by the rebels, which, at that time, consisted of a small slice of bread and about a pint of broth, in which rusty, decayed and spoiled bacon had been boiled, thickened sometimes with a small quantity of rice or beans, twice each day, and this is all.

I have witnessed the issue of those articles to our men, perhaps, a hundred times, and solemnly affirm that I never seen any variation in the quantity or quality above stated. The soup was brought in to the prisoners in wooden buckets, and I have frequently noticed it when the top was covered with white maggots that the process of cooking had forced from the meat and beans. These the prisoners, when not too hungry to wait for their respective allowance, would skim off with an old tin cup, or wooden spoon of their own manufacture, for, be it remembered, that they were robbed of knives, forks, spoons, plates and cups, as well as of their blankets, clothing, hats and boots.

The most of the time, the men above referred to, were confined in Libby, we were allowed to send out and make a few purchases of bread, meat and vegetables; so, that some days, we would have a few crusts of the bread issued to us by the rebels left after our evening meal. These were carefully collected for our men in the room below, and were dropped down to them through a crack in the floor. I have, sometimes, went there with a few crusts of stale bread, and, perhaps, with a few bones, upon which there still remained a little blue beef. At such times I have found as many as could possibly crowd around the hole, standing on tip-toe, their long bony, skeleton-like arms outstretched, ready to grasp in their flesh less fingers any morsel of food, no matter how unpalatable, that we could spare them. One of my friends confined in this room, at this time, says that one evening two of the prisoners were taken down to the hospital, and died before the next morning - *died of utter starvation!*

ESCAPE OF A DEAD YANKEE

It has often been remarked, that Yankee prisoners of war, think of nothing through the day, nor dream of ought in their sleep, but exchange and escape. The following incident would seem to prove that the same hallucination is still with them when dead.

Some time in October, a 'cute Yankee on Belle Isle, managed to get to the hospital before the usual time prescribed by the rebels for taking sick prisoners to that institution for medical treatment, that is, a few hours before the rebel surgeon, who examines them, thinks they will die. Though hundreds of our poor fellows on Belle Isle, in the winter of 1863-'64, "shuffled off this mortal coil," before they were ever removed from the excavations made in the sand to protect them from the chilling blasts of a Virginia winter.

This soldier, that so fortunately got to the hospital, pretended to be sick - *very sick* - and assured the nurse one evening, that it was impossible for him to live until morning. At length, a la Forrest, he commenced counterfeiting the agonies of death. So little attention was given the patients by the rebel surgeon in charge, that no one knew the real condition of the man. The nurse supposed him dying. Finally, he gave a long, difficult drawn gasp, stretched his limbs and seemingly ceased to breathe. Some of the negro attendants connected with the prison, were ordered to carry him to the dead house, and soon the carcass of this live Yankee was deposited by the side of a dead comrade lying there, waiting the morrow to be carted off, and without winding-sheet or coffin interred in an unknown grave. As our hero did not wish this ceremony performed for him just at this time, he quietly took his departure from the house of the dead, and in one week afterwards was inside the Union lines.

CHAPTER V

BELLE ISLE

Through the winter of 1863-'64, some thousands of our men were quartered, or rather turned loose without quarters, inside of a guard line, on this Island, a barren, sandy tract of land several acres in extent, situated in the James river opposite Richmond.

The prisoners on Belle Isle had neither barracks, tents, or shelter of any kind furnished them, until about mid-winter, when a few old worthless tents, too ragged and torn to keep out either wind, rain or snow, perhaps enough to accommodate one-fifth of the men, was given them. In the meantime, however, they had made excavations .in the sand, with pieces of bone, sticks of wood, and in many instances with their fingers alone, as no tools or material to construct a shelter were allowed them, nor any means of living as civilized men, nor way of helping themselves as savages. Their rations· were at all times insufficient, and frequently so foul that starvation itself could not swallow them.

Into these pits made in the sand, our prisoners would huddle like swine in a bed of saw-dust. Lost to all sense of cleanliness, their energies wasted, *hope fled,* their minds demented, they would, during the most inclement weather, lay here for days together, until the calcined sand worked into their skin, producing most frightful consequences, scores and hundreds dying from this cause alone.

The barbarity with which these men were treated would disgrace the wild Arab of the Sahara. No sooner were our men made prisoners, than they were robbed of their blankets, overcoats and money. Many of them were robbed of their hats, shoes, coats and pantaloons, and arrived at Richmond with but their shirts and drawers to cover their nakedness. Terrible as were their sufferings on account of being thus robbed of their clothing, even in the most inclement season of the year, they are as nothing when compared with the misery occasioned for want of food.

About the middle of October, a quantity of clothing was sent by the Government to the prisoners on Belle Isle. General Dow, then a prisoner in Libby, got permission from the rebel authorities 'to go over to the Island and distribute it among the most needy. But

in a state of nudity as they were, with idiotic and childish impatience, they begged of him to bring them something to eat, saying much as they needed clothing they were suffering more for want of food.

These facts seem incredible. Will it, then, be believed that they caught and eat dogs? The editor of the Richmond Examiner not wishing to acknowledge that the Southern people were barbarous enough to reduce their fellow beings to such an extremity, tries to quiet a guilty conscience in the following manner. I quote from the Examiner of January 21st, 1864:

"WARNING TO DOGS, - According to the statement of 'A Citizen,' who writes us , on the subject, Belle Isle, the depot of the Yankee prisoners in Richmond, is unhealthy for dogs - especially well-conditioned dogs. 'The Yankees eat them,' and this our correspondent knows from facts that have come within his knowledge. Several gentlemen on that 'lone barren isle' have lost, recently, their favorite heel-companions, and our correspondent affirms that it is well known to the guard that the Yankees caught, fricasseed and eat them! And that, moreover, the Yankees have begged some citizens to 'let them have their dogs to eat.' Horrible! We are advised, if we doubt the statement of our correspondent, to visit the island and take a dog along, and we will come away alone and convinced.

"All we have to append to this dog story is, that we never did admire Yankee taste in anything; but if they prefer a steak of canine meat "to the rations of beef, bread, potatoes and soup furnished them from the Commissary Department by the prison officials, it is to their liking, not ours. Some animals of a carnivorous nature rather like the flesh of another animal of a like nature. In the above case it is 'dog eat dog,' perhaps."

THE CHICKAMAUGA PRISONERS

Our officers and men captured at Chickamauga, who arrived at Richmond ten days after their capture, had received but twenty hard crackers, a half a pint of eorn meal, and one pound of bacon, during the whole time. And while some of the officers were comfortably clad, the men were in the condition before described, in which prisoners were brought to Richmond. The weather was very chilly during most of the time, and both officers and men, when not on board the cars, were compelled to lie out in the open air, without blankets and without fires.

DEATH IN PRISON

The sick Prisoner. It is impossible to realize the misery conveyed by this expression. Far away from home and the loved ones there - lying on the cold damp ground - no covering but the canopy of heaven; no bedding but a ragged and filthy army blanket; wasting away from consuming fever, or dying of starvation. Oh! how he longs for the gentle hand of a. wife, mother or sister, to bestow on his burning brow and feverish lips a. draught of cool water; and for their sweet words of comfort, encouragement and consolation. On the bed of sickness, no one watches over us with so much care as the wife, mother or sister; their words of kindness and sympathy cheer and comfort us through all affliction.

A Yankee In Rebel Prisons

Death on the field of battle has about it a heroic grandeur that absorbs in a great degree the thoughts of home and friends, and willingly resigns the soldier to a glorious death. But Oh! how horrible to die a prisoner, in the hands of a barbarous enemy!

REBEL HOSPITALS

The rebel hospitals for prisoners were more suitable for horse stables, or sheep pens, than places of habitation for sick and wounded human beings. In the hospital connected with Libby Prison, there were some rudely constructed "bunks," not enough to accommodate more than one-half the patients brought there for treatment. The others were placed in rows on the hard and dirty floor, sometimes without blankets, and frequently without any clothing except their shirts and drawers.

I have seen our men brought from Belle Isle in a dying condition, not from the effects of disease, but starvation. Soon as they arrived at the hospital, they would eagerly ask if they would not get "something to eat now," and in their dying moments convulsively clutch in their bony fingers a piece of bread, and try to convey it to their mouths, I am fully convinced, from personal experience and observation, that nine tenths of our men who died in the rebel prisons of the South, in the last two years, were brought to their death by starvation and exposure. Even in the hospitals they received no nutritious or palatable diet. At the Andersonville prison hospitals, the diet of the patients was corn meal gruel, corn bread, and occasionally a little boiled rice, served with salt.

Those that were fortunate enough to get to the hospitals at all, were not taken there until in a dying condition. I have seen scores of our men brought to the hospital in Richmond, from Belle Isle, who were carried out dead within an hour after their names were registered.

A Yankee In Rebel Prisons

After our men were removed from Belle Isle to Danville, Virginia, the ravages of disease was still more terrible. I have no correct information in regard to the number of prisoners that died there, but give the following from the Richmond Dispatch of January 26th, in reference to the fatality among them:

"The Yankee Prisoners At Danville, - The Danville *Register* says the small-pox continues to spread among the Yankee prisoners there. The number of cases is now three hundred. The virus furnished by their own Government having been generally administered, the progress of the disease may be checked. The fatality among the prisoners from this and other maladies is very great. Several wagon loads are hauled out to the graveyard every day from the general hospital, besides those who die of small-pox"

THE EXAMINER COUNSELS MURDER

In October, 1863, the rebel authorities resolved to remove the prisoners from Belle Isle, to some point not so liable to "Yankee raids." The frequent demonstration of Union cavalry up the peninsula, coming sometimes almost within sight of the throne of Jefferson the First, (and last,) suggesting to the mind of the rebel Secretary of War, the fact, that Richmond was not the safest place in the Confederacy for prisoners of war, and that "beast" Butler might send force enough to enter Richmond and release them.

From an article in the Examiner of October 30th, 1863, in reference to the removal of the prisoners from Richmond, I make the following extract:

"The proper authorities are debating the question of the removal of the twelve thousand Yankee prisoners from Richmond to some other point. * * * * Danville, or some location on the James River Canal, are spoken of. We are glad the question has been started, and the citizens of Richmond will do all in their power to help them to a decision.

The Yankee Government, under the laws of civilized warfare, are entitled to these men, and if they will not take them, let them be put where cold weather and scant fare will thin them out in accordance with the laws of nature."

In Courts of Justice the accessory to a crime is always considered, in a greater or less degree, guilty, and frequently the same punishment awarded that the principal receives. Yet the editor of the sacrilegious sheet containing the above, Mr. Pollard, after advising the inhuman murder of Union prisoners of war, was treated, during his captivity in the North, with the greatest consideration and respect - was finally paroled, and remained some time with his friends in the city of Baltimore, receiving the kindest attention from Union citizens (?) of that place. How humiliating to the brave men (if any still survive,) whose murder he advised!

THE CONTRAST

While our men in Southern prisons were dying from starvation and exposure, the rebels in Northern prisons fared sumptuously every day; had good quarters, plenty of fuel, and received the respects and civilities due them as prisoners of war.

At Johnson's Island, where the rebel officers were confined, the prisoners had almost as many accommodations as at a first class hotel. The extract given below from a rebel letter shows how they fare on that "bleak wintry Isle." The letter was written by a returned rebel surgeon to a gentleman in Augusta, Georgia, who had a son on the Island, and published in the Richmond Enquirer, from which this extract is taken:

A Yankee In Rebel Prisons

"The sleeping accommodations are very comfortable, consisting of a bunk, with straw bed, and if the individual has no blanket one is furnished, and he is allowed to buy as many more as he wants. Every room has a good stove, and furnished with a sufficiency of wood, which the prisoners have to saw for themselves after it is brought to their doors - by the way, a very good exercise. The prison consist of thirteen large buildings of wood. The space of ground enclosed is sixteen acres, of which the prisoners have full privilege to exercise in, to sing Southern National songs, to hurrah for Jeff Davis, and to play at ball, or any other game they may see fit.

"The rations are exactly the same as issued to the garrison, consisting of fresh beef, pork, baker's bread, sugar, coffee, beans, hominy, vinegar, salt, soap and candles. Besides this, up to the time I left, there was a sutlers store inside the enclosure, from which we could obtain any kind of vegetables and meats, or nick-nacks, that we chose. We could purchase clothing of any kind, or anything we wanted. Clothing and eatables of all kinds were allowed to be sent to the prisoners, by their friends in the North, in any quantity: money also without stint.

"When I left the Island, the excitement about the release of the prisoners by a force from Canada was at its highest pitch, necessarily causing the garrison to be reinforced. This coming so suddenly, found the commissary stores on the Island deficient, and the rations for both prisoners and garrison were somewhat curtailed. The sutler was also sent away and the prisoners still more restricted. I hope, however, before this time, things are pursuing the even tenor of their way, and that the prisoners are enjoying themselves as heretofore. We had the privilege of writing as many letters as .we chose, and when we chose, of course subject to certain restrictions; we could purchase writing materials in any quantity.

"The officers over the prisoners have, at all times, conducted themselves as gentlemen, and have been very kind and lenient; nor do they suffer the prisoners to be insulted or abused in any way."

If our Union soldiers, prisoners at the South, had received such kind treatment as this, the sixteen thousand brave men, now sleeping beneath the cold damp earth in the vicinity of Andersonville, Georgia, would now have been alive, and at home, to gladden and make happy their wives, mothers, children and friends, and ready with strong arms and brave hearts to defend their country.

CHAPTER VI

WINTER IN LIBBY

We will now return to the Libby. We have been here, oh! how many wretched, dreary days! Have seen the fields and forest on the opposite side of the swift waters of the James put on the green robes of spring - the sultry summer months come and pass away- then the autumn frosts, robbing the old trees of their green leaves, and ·fields and gardens of their rich carpeting of plants and bright hued flowers, The beauteous garb in which the warm sun of spring and summer attired nature, has faded and decayed, Hoary headed winter is upon us, his chilling blasts whistle between the bars of the grated and narrow windows; comes in and pierces the emaciated forms of the half clad prisoners, warning them that their own ingenuity and labor must be brought into requisition for a slight taste of comfort, and even perhaps for the preservation of life. The ragged, filthy blankets that lay untouched in a heap in one corner of the prison during the hot summer months, when the inmates sought sleep *en deshabille*, on the hard and naked floor, now that we are not so particular, are readily made use of, regardless of the numerous vermin that inhabit them. About half were thus supplied with blankets of the above description..

About this time we were recommended to send home for blankets, clothing, and such other articles as we would need for our comfort during the winter; we were assured that all such articles would be promptly delivered to us immediately after their arrival. This is glorious news! but will the rebels keep their faith? they have made frequent promises of future favors, but these have been as often broken; but hunger and cold stares us in the face, and we trust them again. The first installments are at once delivered, as per agreement, and by the greatest industry and ingenuity our prison abode soon wears, in a slight degree, the aspect of home, though of all places on the broad earth the most unlike that sweet haven of rest, happiness and comfort. Our worn and cast-off clothing is manufactured into curtains; and hung in the windows; they keep out all of the light and some of the cold air, but the darkness even of a dungeon was preferable to the suffering we would otherwise have to endure from the effects of cold.

It must not be thought, from this description, that the prisoners quietly resigned themselves to a state of somnolency, and stowed their bodies away like dormant animals until the coming spring; though many nights when suffering with hunger and cold, I have laid down in my place on the floor and devoutly prayed that I might remain in the unconsciousness of sleep until the day of deliverance from my wretched condition.

INSIDE VIEW OF LIBBY

In the preceding pages I have given a general description of the treatment, rations and quarters we received from the hands of the rebel officials. I shall now attempt to give, in detail, an account of the daily round of duties, occupations and amusements of the prisoners.

With the first gray dawn of the morning, the sleepers lying on the floor in uneasy slumbers, side by side, and heel to head, are aroused to consciousness by the stentorian voice of a certain colored "gentleman," well known to the inmates of Libby as "Old Ben," crying out, "All four ob de morning papers. Talagraphic dispatches from ebery whar. Rise, gentlemen, and buy de morning news. Great news from de Rappahannock. Great news from Charleston. Great news from de south-west and de east-west. Are all de gemmen 'commodated with de morning news? I'se bound for to trabel." He brought copies of the daily Richmond papers, each a small half sheet of brown, dingy paper, generally containing but little that we could regard as reliable. They usually had a leading article filled with the most exaggerated statements and falsehoods of "Yankee barbarity," and thoroughly imbued with the most uncompromising hate of the Union, and of all who remained loyal to the Government. But alas! for poor Ben's career as a disseminator of "talagraphic dispatches" and "news from ebery whar," to Yankee officers. He was charged by the prison officials with trading with us for "green-backs," and other disloyal acts, and at once prohibited vending "all four of de morning papers" in the prison.

Scarcely would the strong brazen notes of "Ben" cease to resound through the prison, than the nasal twang of George, one of the prison attaches, would ascend the stairway, ordering us to fall in for roll call. If any still lingered in the embrace of Morpheus, this was a sufficient signal for the immediate expulsion of that mythological personage, twenty minutes only being allowed after the musical notes of the above voice fell on the ear for all to go to the east room; and woe to the unlucky wight who failed to be there within the time specified, as he would be immediately sentenced by one of the prison officials to stand under guard, on the floor of the cook room, for four hours.

After we had been crowded and jammed into the above room as thick as bees in a hive, we were counted out one by one. We had roll again in the afternoon; thus nearly eleven hundred human beings were packed twice each day into a single room, where they had often to remain for an hour each time, and breathe the impure and unwholesome air thus generated.

PRISONERS COOKING

After morning roll call, the next business in order for the now thoroughly aroused prisoners, is for those whose turn it is to act as cooks for their respective messes, to commence their culinary labors, which consisted in boiling a little rice, which was served up with salt. Then the rattle of cooking utensils, the slamming of stove doors, the crowding around the fires of a hundred men, each with his tin cup, intent on preparing for himself some extra dish, affords a lively and amusing scene. Each mess of twenty enjoyed its privilege of the mess kettles and tables in regular order, and one succeeds another in the greatest rapidity practicable.

After arrangements were made for the prisoners to receive provisions from the North, the services of good cooks were in great demand, and it was a frequent occurrence to see one of the fortunate recipients of a portion of the " *good things from home*," perambulating the different apartments of the prison, enquiring" who wants to cook for my box." And among those who were living, or rather *starving* on Confederate rations, there were always enough who would willingly become the servants of their brother officers for the sake of something good to eat. But when all became supplied, these knights of the pots and pans resolved to cook for their own boxes; consequently each officer, Brigadier as well as Lieutenant, was at length compelled to do his own cooking. The avidity with which they would pour over the household department of old magazines and newspapers in search of receipts for preparing various dishes, was no less astonishing than the rapidity with which they became adepts in this branch of house keeping. Should the wives of any have doubts on this point, they have only to send them to the kitchen to prepare a breakfast or dinner, and they will be at once amply convinced of their proficiency in the art,

AMUSEMENTS

Some pass the hours in reading, writing, or in games, among which chess, checkers, and the various games with cards, are included. Nearly all seem to find enjoyment and consolation in smoking, and a person of sensitive olfactories who disliked tobacco, if in Libby, was a martyr, with no possibility of escape. He must eat it in his rice and corn bread, and drink it in his coffee, inhale it every breath, and experience no relief till lost in the unconsciousness which sleep brought to his offended senses.

Among the variety of pursuits and amusements, music claims no small share of attention, and groups may here and there be found, intent upon rendering, in most melodious accents, the choicest selections from Mozart, Handel, and other masters of sacred song. In other places, proficients upon the violin discourse Ethiopian melodies, to which some charmed listeners are keeping time, giving most lively motion to their pedal extremities. Others are busily engaged in manufacturing ornaments from the bones of the blue beef that furnished us food. Many of these were specimens of mechanical skill truly worthy of admiration. Here were finger rings of exquisite workmanship; crosses, inlaid with hard rubber cut from the back of a pocket comb; napkin rings wrought with the most elaborate designs; miniature toilet tables, &c., in great profusion.

PRISONERS' LETTERS

Communicating with the loved ones at home was our chief source of enjoyment. A most happy privilege while it lasted! But this simple means of gratification was finally, almost totally denied to us. And the following order, issued by the commandant of the prison, I give it *verbatim et literatim*:

OFFICE C. S. MILITARY PRISON,
Richmond, Va., February 14th, 1864.

Hereafter prisoners won't be allowed to ,write no letters to go to the so called United States, of more than six lines in length and only one letter per week.

By command of

THOS. P. TURNER,
Major C. S. A.

"Letters from home!" Oh, what a thrill of pleasure this announcement would send to the heart of the weary prisoner! Could the wives mothers and sisters of our soldiers realize the exstatic joy that swells the bosoms of husbands, sons and brothers, on receipt of their tender and affectionate letters - the hope, courage and high resolves with which they animate them, their fair hands would certainly be more frequently engaged in this work of love. And ladies, take my advice – write to your loved ones often! You have no idea of the good you can accomplish in this way, and at so little expense.

I have seen men on the bloody field, and in hospitals, their lives passing fast away from the effects of ghastly wounds or consuming fevers, whose last lingering gaze rested fondly on these missives of love. Truly, they brought hope and consolation in this most trying hour!

The affable and genial Lieutenant Knaggs was our Postmaster. On the arrival of the mail he would select some elevated spot, or, perhaps, take a position astride one of the naked beams in the "upper west room," when he was immediately surrounded by the entire population of Libby, each one anxiously hoping that his name might be first called. · But never, at one time, were all suplied, and many, always, returned disappointed and gloomy to their chosen spot, wondering why no letters from wife or mother.

A Yankee In Rebel Prisons

"FRESH FISH"

Familiar in the mouths of the inhabitants of Libby as "household words." Heard in the gray of morning when the disconsolate crowd of prisoners just arrived, await in the street in front of the prison the scaling process, which always takes place before they are packed away for safe keeping, Heard, also, in the dead of night, when the sleepers turn over in their blankets to curse the fresh fish for disturbing their slumbers at such unseasonable hours, the poor fresh fish standing, meanwhile, a disconsolate group, wondering why no better accommodations have been made for their reception; and, after fruitless conjectures, depositing themselves on the bare and dirty floor, and sink to sleep, after exhausting their minds speculating on the magnanimity of the" Southern Chivalry."

The cry of "fresh fish" is a slang phrase, and never to be forgotten by the unfortunate whose arrival it announces, and who, should it be his fate to make his debut in Libby when the inmates are not asleep, is immediately surrounded by a gaping crowd of awkward auditors, eager to learn what is transpiring in the outer world, when the hapless fresh fish have to answer repeatedly the scores of questions propounded in rapid succession by hundreds of old .fish; and one who could pass through the ordeal without losing his equanimity, was certainly possessed of the patience of Job, and the affability of Chesterfield,

Among the leading inquiries made of the new arrivals, were the following: "'Where were you captured ?" "Did the rebs get your greenbacks?" "How did you hide your watch?" "What does the Northern press say about the exchange?" Thus, from the constant advent of "fresh fish," and the occasional receipt of a letter six: lines in length from friends in the North, we were kept a little better informed in regard to what was transpiring outside of Libby, than if we had been residents of Jupiter or the moon.

EXCHANGE

At all hours of the day discussions and speculations in regard to the resumption of the "cartel," might be heard among the prisoners whose thoughts seemed to dwell constantly on the scenes and affections of home.

Libby was certainly the most prolific place in the world for rumors, not even excepting the most gossiping sewing circle ever established in a country village. Consequent.ly there were many of these that daily went the rounds to elate or depress the mind of the prisoner, who, whatever else he might do or think, ceased not to long for the happy hour which should place him again under the "Star Spangled Banner," and return him once more to the society of loved ones at home. Examples of these ever-recurring, hope-inspiring and depressing agents, were the following:

"Commissioners of Exchange met yesterday, and effected a cartel! All to be exchanged immediately!"

Then, in the same hour, purporting to come from the same official: "Commissioners could not agree! No exchange probable for months to come!" The negro question prevents all exchange!"

Then: "The negro question has never been in issue!"

One comes directly from the commandant of the prison and informs us: "That we will be here only a short time longer."

Another says: "It has been advised from the same authority that we had better send home and get a supply of clothing and provisions!"

And so wears away the day, till at length the sable curtains of night again cast their shadows over the crowded rooms.

NIGHT IN LIBBY

Some of the most ludicrous incidents in Libby life occur after all its inhabitants have arranged themselves, each in his chosen spot upon the floor, with his army blanket around him. Then commences a succession of conundrums, questions and replies, technically called the catechism. This embodied a general censor-ship of the habits, opinions or peculiarities of whatever kink, of any who might attract special attention. And among such a collection of persons, of such diversity of opinions, and such a variety of habits, enough could always be found to furnish means for an hour of uproarious hilarity. Such as the following questions would be proposed:

"Why ought the best of English poetry to emanate from this room?" Because we have a Spencer and a Burns here, and they live in a: garret - a poet's usual abode.

"Who stole Mosley's hash?" General Dow.

"Who offered to enlist in the rebel army if he could be released from prison?" Goldsboro.

"Who put soap in the small mess kettle?" Piper.

"Who said they got more meat than they could eat?" Ely and Sanderson.

"Who sold his boots to buy extra mutton chops?" Ely.

"How does Libby differ from another public institution in Philadelphia?" That is a *Northern home* for friendless children; this is a friendless home for Northern children, &c., &c.

At length all seem satisfied, and sleep and silence - except the sub-base of heavy snoring from many upturned noses - reigns supreme till the coming dawn of another day. Thus, it will be seen, that live Yankees, even when prisoners in rebeldom, and subject to all the discomforts which semi-barbarism can impose, will be Yankees still, and will find amusement in the exercise of the mental vivacity peculiar to the race.

CHAPTER VII

ESCAPE OF ANDERSON AND SKELTON

We have been now eight months incarcerated within the gloomy walls of Libby. And so closely have we been guarded, and so securely closed and barred the doors and windows, that escape seems to be impossible, no one has yet attempted it, though many schemes have been proposed and canvassed by different parties, but finally dismissed as impracticable. Captain M. T. Anderson, of the Fifty-First Indiana Volunteers, at length resolved on the novel expedient of feigning sickness, and thus get to the hospital, so that he would have an opportunity of conversing with the sentinels posted around that part of the building; and, as he had still some money about him that be had smuggled into the prison, he hoped to be able to bribe them to let him pass out. The influence of Uncle Sam's "greenbacks" over the rebel guards was entirely satisfactory, and the Captain at once set about making arrangements for his departure from Libby. The first thing was to find, among his fellow-prisoners, a suitable companion to accompany him, one who would be willing to brave any danger in order to gain their freedom. One to the Captain's liking was found in the person of Lieutenant J. F. Skelton, of the Seventeenth Iowa Volunteers. The hospital room is on the ground ftoor in the east end of the Libby prison. The cook room for the sick was in the basement or cellar immediately under it, and from this they determined to make their exit. There were four sentinels on the south side of the building, and three on the east end, and one opposite and directly in front of the small door through which they intended passing out; two of these sentinels they succeeded in bribing, and trusted to their activity and good luck to evade the vigilance of the others.

On the night of December 11th, all arrangements being completed, they commenced putting their plans into execution. With a large meat cleaver, they cut the bars from the door before mentioned, and just at the hour of ten they swung it back on its hinges, and were stepping from bondage to liberty, when the corporal of the guard was called by one of the sentinels. Hope sank within them; their first impression was that the guard had betrayed them; all their fond hopes of liberty and freedom were instantly dispelled. But soon the corporal made his "rounds," and all was again quiet. The time of night was called by sentinel number one, and passed successively from right to left; the backs of the sentinels are now turned on the door; the captain and his companion instantly see their advantage, and quicker than I can describe it they again swing the shutter back, jump out and over the guardline, and are free. They proceed down Carey street towards Rocketts, coolly and slowly as if traversing some old familiar path of by-gone days. About thirty minutes walking brought them to the outskirts of the city, and in sight of the forts and works surrounding it; knowing that pickets would be stationed near by, they left the main road and entered a deep ravine, in which they remained until they passed through the works and pickets defending Richmond. They now felt that they had gained their liberty; gloomy walls of a loathsome prison no longer encompassed them. Yet it required patience, toil, and suffering and caution, to reach the Union lines through an enemies country of nearly one hundred miles in extent, with every public and by-road closely guarded and patrolled. In consequence of their limited knowledge of the country, and the darkness of the night, which prevented them from directing their course by a small compass in their possession they lost the route, and wandered round until daylight, to find they were only five or six miles from the city of Richmond. To attempt traveling during daylight was certain recapture; so they concealed themselves in some thick underbrush, though here they did not feel entirely safe, for they lay within a mile of the rebel camp, Confederate soldiers constantly passing back and forth, and within a few yards of where the fugitives lay.

Hour after hour they watched the road for some wandering slave to pass by, knowing well that Union soldiers could always put implicit confidence in the black man; they would, therefore, make known to him who they were, and get the exact locality of their present position, also the situation of the rebel camps at Bottom's Bridget across the Chickahominy river. Late in the evening the sound of a wagon was heard coming down the road; they cautiously crawled to within a few feet of where it would pass, and anxiously awaited its approach; it soon came in sight, and to their great joy they discovered that the team was driven by a negro; soon as he came up he was promptly halted, whereupon he drew up his mules with a loud *whoa*, but what was the surprise of the fugitives to see a white man jump out of the wagon. They had no idea of finding an individual in this locality of his color that was a friend; consequently to deceive him was their first thought. He inquired what they wanted, and was answered that they were in search of a runaway slave, that he had been tracked to that neighborhood when all trace of him was lost. The explanation seemed satisfactory, and like a true Virginian he promised to do all in his power to intercept the runaway, and master and slave, with the team, passed on very much to the joy and delight of our escaped Yankees.

Immediately after dark they again started on their journey northward, taking the Williamsburg pike towards Bottom's Bridge, passing directly in front of the headquarters of the commanding. officer of the troops at that place. Before reaching the bridge it began raining so furiously, and was so dark, that to proceed further on the way was impossible; and they again lay down without shelter, overcoats or blankets, to pass away the long tedious hours of a stormy night. Daybreak at last became visible in the east, and they determined to travel, regardless of danger, and started in a northeast course, which they followed until they reached the middle of the White Oak swamp; they then changed to an eastern course, and all of that day (the 13th of December) they waded often waist deep through mud and water; but nothing daunted or discouraged they kept on, striving for liberty and freedom, willingly periling their lives to reach the land where the starry flag is the emblem of the free. About sunset of this day they crossed the Chickahominy on a fallen tree which had blown down, and fortunately lodged across the river just at the point where they first struck the banks of the stream.

Being now tired, hungry, and footsore, from excessive exertion, having traveled nearly twenty miles through the swamp, they again deposited themselves on the cold wet ground for a few hours sleep and rest, but it was another fearful stormy night of wind and rain, and sleet, consequently to sleep was impossible and at the first gray streak of morning light they proceeded on their weary march. They bad not gone far before they were discovered in the road by a rebel soldier; they at once determined to defend themselves as best they could, in case of an attempt on the part of the scout to capture them. But again fortune favored them, and the scout passed by without speaking. They now left all roads, both highways and by-paths, and traveled exclusively through forests, swamps and fields, and about ten o'clock they came in contact with a negro girl in the woods, gathering up dry leaves for bedding; they questioned her in regard to roads and different localities, but she could give them no information. When they informed her that they were Yankee officers, she seemed to experience the greatest anxiety for their safety, and when they started off she admonished them to hurry, for, said she, "massa will be here 'drecly now." In consequence of this information, they pushed on at a double quick for several miles.

Late that night they reached Haw creek, and after refreshing themselves with some corn bread and bacon, lay down to sleep as usual, with the heavens for their only covering, and mother earth their bed, but sleepy and fatigued as they were they could not sleep for the extreme pain they suffered from cold. Early next morning they were again on the road, weary and exhausted from loss of sleep, but still they bend their course northward; they have suffered too long in rebel prisons to give up and be taken back, as long as they could march even a single rod per day, After proceeding about a mile, they discovered two horsemen approaching; they quickly concealed themselves in the brush, and awaited for them to pass by, but when they came within a short distance it was discovered that the riders were negroes, which put the fugitives quite at ease, and they at once informed the slaves that they were "Yankee officers," trying to reach the Union lines. This was very much of a surprise to the " darkies," and caused each of them to disclose a huge amount of ivory; but their joy was quickly changed to fear and anxiety for the safety of their Northern friends, and they at once volunteered to aid them to the extent of their ability; the kindly proffer was at once accepted, In accordance with instructions from their dusky protectors, they remained concealed in this vicinity until night; one of the negroes then Came and piloted them to his friend's house, where they were furnished with a warm meal; the negro, while they were eating, brought a cart, the bed of which was filled with corn blades, around to the door, and notified them that all was ready, and they were soon securely stored away beneath the fodder, in this position they rode eight miles, where they stopped at a negro hut, the dwelling of a friend of the guide; here they were almost compelled by the urgency of the black folks to partake of another supper, This was as far as prudent to go with the horse and cart, but the faithful guide piloted them on foot for three miles further, and after giving them the most careful directions in regard to the roads and country, with throbbing heart and streaming eyes bid his Yankee friends good-bye.

The escaped prisoners were now about eleven miles from the Union lines, so, with light hearts they pushed rapidly on, knowing from the description given them by the negro, how to recognize the country in the vicinity of the Federal pickets. After three hours' hard marching, they thought it time to be near the boys in blue. They advanced but a few rods further, when they were suddenly ordered to halt, an order they very promptly executed; by looking in the direction from whence came the sound of the voice, they could just see the figures of three mounted men with presented guns. It was so dark that their uniforms could not be distinguished, therefore they could not discover whether they were friends or foes. "Who goes there ?" was the challenge of the watchful sentry, which was answered by " friends." "Advance, friends," was the next order. "To whom shall we advance," was the reply of the careful fugitives. The soldiers on duty proved to be Union pickets, a happy discovery to Captain Anderson and his companion. They were again beneath the protecting folds of the old flag. Every attention and kindness was shown them by the officer of the guard, and next morning he conducted them to the head-quarters of the Post Commandant, who kindly furnished them transportation to Fortress Monroe, where they met General Butler; he received them very cordially, and made many inquiries in regard to the condition of our unfortunate prisoners in Richmond.

Each spent a few weeks at home, recruiting his health and exhausted energies before taking the field; since when they have zealously endeavored to repay the rebels for their kind treatment while prisoners of war.

THE COUNCIL OF FIVE

In October a plan was projected for a general outbreak of the prisoners confined in Libby. The whole arrangement, and every thing connected with it, was gotten up on a well digested plan, which was to be executed in systematic order. Colonel A. D. Streight, of the Fifty-First Indiana Volunteers, was chosen to be chief in command, and Colonels Powell, Rose and Ely, to be commanders of brigades.

The organization was known as the "Council of Five," from the fact of the members being classed off in clubs, each of which contained that number, on account of it being impossible for all to meet together for the purpose of transacting business; for by so doing, secrecy, which was absolutely essential to the success of the undertaking, could not be maintained.

The objects embraced in the enterprise, was not only to secure our own freedom, but after we had seized and overpowered the guard doing duty at the prison, to take their arms and march to the tobacco warehouses where a number of our soldiers were imprisoned, release them and proceed to the arsenal, take possession, and arm and equip ourselves with the guns and accouterments found there; then release all the prisoners confined in and around Richmond, form them into companies, regiments and brigades, and, if possible, take prisoners Jefferson Davis and his Cabinet, and other leading rebels the in the city, and then march en masse down the Peninsula until we should arrive within our own lines.

From a Union lady with whom communication was had, through a negro, who was allowed access to the prison for the purpose of scrubbing the floor and carrying out the slops collected in the kitchen, we had the most correct and reliable information in regard to the number of troops in the vicinity of the city, the number and kind of arms and accoutrements, and amount of ammunition in the arsenal and other places in Richmond.

Notwithstanding every member of the organization was bound by the most solemn oath to preserve the strictest secrecy, its existence was discovered by some of the inmates of the prison, not connected with the enterprise, and who were more friendly to rebel officials than to their fellow prisoners, and by them treacherously revealed to the authorities having us in charge, who, acting on the information thus gained from the traitors confined with us as Union prisoners of war, immediately doubled the guard, and planted cannon bearing from various points on the prison; General Pickett's division was also ordered to the vicinity of Richmond for the purpose of overpowering any attempt at an outbreak..

It was but a few days before the time designated for the execution of the enterprise, that this discovery was made to the rebel authorities; but measures were so promptly taken by them to meet, and if possible prevent it, (all of which were known to us,) that the project was at once abandoned as impracticable.

The abandonment of the scheme was not yet known to the Commandant of the prison; and that worthy, thinking no doubt to put an end to all attempts of the kind, deliberately resolved on the following plan to murder Colonel Streight, who was known to be the leader. He addressed a note to Colonel Streight, saying that we were fools for remaining in prison, and that if two wished to pass out that night they could do so by paying the guard on a certain post one hundred dollars in greenbacks, and two silver watches. This was placed in the hands of the sentinel on a certain post, who, according to his instructions, threw it in the prison through one of the windows. Colonel Streight, not once suspecting any foul play or treachery, and thinking it only a plan of speculation on the part of the guard, immediately prepared to take advantage of the opportunity thus offered to regain his liberty.

The Colonel borrowed the money, and Captain B. C. G. Read, of the Third Ohio Volunteer's, procured the watches, and at the appointed time both proceeded to the window designated, and with the aid of a blanket, descended on the outside to the ground, handed the guard the money and watches, and passed outside the sentry's beat. They proceeded only a few steps, when they were fired upon by a squad of rebel soldiers, (fortunately without injury to either,) who immediately surrounded them and conducted them back within the gloomy walls of the prison they had just left, and they were at once placed in one of the dungeons in the basement of the Libby, where their situation and suffering was most horrible.

The reader can judge of their condition from the following communication, addressed by Colonel Streight while in the cell, to the United States Commissioner for Exchange of Prisoners. It was written with a pencil on a slip of paper torn from his memorandum book, and passed through a hole cut in the floor to one of his officers in the prison above, who copied it and sent it through clandestinely by a surgeon who was exchanged and going North.

IN THE CELL, RICHIMOND, VIRGINIA,
December 22d, 1863.

GENERAL: - I have the honor to report to you the situation that Captain B. C. G. Read, Third Ohio Volunteers, and myself, are in, and the circumstances connected with our being here. On the eighteenth instant I received a note, stating that we were fools for staying in prison, and that if two of us wished to leave at three o'clock the following morning, we could do so by paying the sentinel on a certain post one hundred dollars in greenbacks and two silver watches, as a compensation for the risk of being detected. I borrowed the money, and Captain Read procured the watches, and at the appointed hour we proceeded to the designated place; the money and watches were handed over, and we were allowed to pass out. But no sooner were we outside the guard line, than an indiscriminate fire was opened on us by a party of the prison attaches, (seven in number,) headed by Lieutenant LaTouche, Adjutant of the prison. We were seized and ironed, and placed in this cell on bread and ,vater. There was no attempt on the part of the prison authorities to conceal the fact, that they deliberately laid the plan, and seemed to consider it a smart trick. I leave you to judge whether it was not a deliberate plot to rob and murder us.

The cell in which we are placed is in one corner of the cellar of Libby prison. We were without fire until yesterday, though it was most bitter cold, and now we are nearly suffocated with smoke. I cannot describe to you the filth, nor the loathing stench with which we are surrounded. The cellar is filled with old rubbish, and to all appearances has not been cleaned for years, consequently the number of rats and mice is beyond computation. How long the prison authorities will keep us here I have no idea; but certain it is, we can not survive it long. I have stated that we were reduced to bread and water fare; I will add that what we get for bread is of such a quality that we, as yet, have been unable to eat it.

I trust you will take such measures as will compel these men to treat us as prisoners of war. I will further state for your information, that when I came here I found six of our soldiers who had been here one week. They were taken out yesterday. Some measures should be adopted to prevent such barbarities as are daily being practiced on our officers and men.

I send you this privately. They have refused me permission to write.

Very respectfully, your obedient servant,

A. D. STREIGHT,
Colonel Fifty-First Indiana Volunteers.

To Brigadier General S. A. Meredith,
Commissioner for Exchange of Prisoners.

The following, from the Richmond Enquirer, furnished by the prison officials, gives their version of the affair, from which it will be seen that although they blame the above parties with making the proposition to the guard, they do not try to keep secret the fact that it was a plot to rob our men of their money and valuables, also to murder them, should the least resistance be offered to their recapture.

ESCAPE AND RECAPTURE .- The Yankee officers confined in the Libby prison, have, on several occasions lately, made unsuccessful attempts to escape from that institution. The desire to escape seems to have grown with them since the successful evacuation of the premises by Captain Anderson and Lieutenant Skelton, heretofore noticed, and which was produced by bribing the sentinel on duty at the time. On Friday evening, a sentinel on duty in the rear of Libby prison, was sounded by two officers on the subject of an escape, which they wished to effect at three and a half o'clock, .that night. He agreed to their proposals; they promising to give him a one hundred dollar green back and two watches for his services.

:Major Turner, being notified of the affair, directed the sentinel to let the parties escape and receive the bonus for so doing, and that he would take care they did not get very far off: Accordingly, at three and a half o'clock, a rear window of the middle tenement of the Libby establishment, was raised, a blanket rope extended to the ground, and two men descended. Hastily approaching the sentinel, they handed him the green back and two silver watches, and were making remarkable good time, when they were hailed by Lieutenant La Touche, and commanded to stop. This accelerated their speed in the direction of Rocketts, but they had not gone very far when the guard, which had been posted, closed around the fugacious yankees, and their capture was complete. On the approach of Lieutenant LaTouche, he recognized the notorious Colonel A. D. Streight and his Adjutant, Lieutenant Reed. They were conducted back to the Libby, furnished with substantial irons, and put in the dungeon of the prison, where they were at last accounts, "chewing the cud of sweet and bitter fancies." The Yankee officers had, previous to the attempt of Streight, determined to celebrate Christmas night by a grand musical entertainment. Whether their purpose will be affected by Streight's proceedings, remains to be seen."

They were kept in the cell twenty-one days, confined on a diet of coarse, half-baked corn bread, and water, and heavily ironed, and closely guarded during the whole of the time They had no means of personal cleanliness, neither , water for washing, basin or combs, nor change of clothing being furnished them; consequently, when they made their appearance in their old quarters, in the upper part of the building, they were so haggard and polluted with filth as to be scarcely recognizable by their former comrades. When first taken to the cell, the Colonel requested a box to sit on; they would not allow him to have it. He desired them to clean the filth out of his dungeon-they refused. He then asked them to take off his irons and furnish him with a broom that he might do it himself; this privilege was also denied.

.   A guard was kept constantly in front of the grated door of the cell, to watch every motion they made, lest they should attempt, by some means, to relieve themselves of their jewels.

Among civilized people it is a recognized principle of military law, to be the duty of a prisoner of war to escape from the hands of the enemy if possible, in fact to make every effort in his power to do so. For such attempts at escape, his captors have the right to confine him in more secure quarters. But neither law nor the usages of civilized nations recognize the right of punishment, by confinement in dark, dank, filthy dungeons, or a reduction of food to an insufficient quantity to sustain life and health, or other means of torture. Yet our ·officers and men, when recaptured, after an attempted escape, were subjected by these rebels to the most inhuman cruelties.

JOHN MORGAN VISITS LIBBY

A few days after Colonel Streight was taken from the dungeon and restored to his old quarters with the rest of the prisoners, the famous, or rather, infamous, General John H. Morgan, who had just escaped from the Ohio penitentiary, paid a visit to Libby. He was accompanied by the rebel General A. P. Hill, the Mayor of the city of Richmond, Joseph Mayo, and other rebel notables. They were conducted through the different apartments of the prison by one of the officials in charge, who introduced them to several of the prisoners with whom he had become acquainted, including General Neal Dow and Colonel Streight, both of whom received the great rebel bandit with becoming dignity and respect. There was no expression of gratification and delight, or show of admiration manifested by any of the prisoners for the great guerrilla; though one of the Richmond papers, the following morning, contained an article saying that the "Kentucky officers expressed the most unqualified delight at seeing the favorite son of their own State, not only delighted to see him, but also delighted that he had escaped from prison and was once more at liberty;" a statement in which there was about as much truth as in the following, taken from the Richmond Examiner, where it says General Dow's opinions had changed considerable during his confinement, in favor of the South:

"General Morgan's Visit to the Libby Prison. – On Saturday, the city's guest, General John H. Morgan, escorted by His Honor, Joseph Mayo, Mayor of Richmond, Acting Adjutant General R. A. Alston, Mr. Bruce, Member of Congress, from Kentucky, and a number or others, paid a visit. to the Libby prison, where an opportunity was afforded them of inspecting that famous receptacle of Union sentiment and the parties who give it vitality. These, in round numbers, foot up considerably over a thousand - an aggregate sufficient to make a most respectable regiment, so far as mere numbers are concerned. General Morgan and party arrived at the prison about eleven o'clock, and, on making their wishes known, were immediately conducted on a tour of inspection. General .Morgan, on arriving up stairs, where the prisoners "most do congergate," was immediately conducted into the presence of the "author of the Maine Liquor Law," the whilom Brigadier General Neal Dow. An introduction took place, when Morgan observed, with one of those inimitable smiles for which he is so noted, "General Dow, I am very happy to see you here; or, rather, since you are here, I am happy to see you looking so well." Dow's natural astute-ness and Yankee ingenuity came to his aid, and he quickly replied, without apparent, embarrassment, "General Morgan, I congratulate you on your escape; I cannot say that I am glad you did escape, but, since you did, I am pleased to see you here." The conversation then became general between the two, during the progress of which Dow admitted that his views of the South, its people, and their treatment of prisoners of war had undergone a considerable change for' the better within the last few months.

General Morgan also had an interview with the notorious Colonel Streight, who had, several days previous to his visit, been released from close confinement for attempting to escape from prison, and restored to his old place amongst the other officers,

While .at the Libby General Morgan visited the hospital attached to the prison, and gave high praise to surgeon Wilkins and his co-laborers for their efficient conduct. The General said the hospitals were all that could be desired, and kept in true military style.

The only drawback to the pleasant reflections induced by their visit was the existence of a fact which unconsciously leaked out during its progress. On several occasions lately, owing to the insufficiency and want of industry or attention on the part of the quartermaster charged with the duty of furnishing fuel for the use of the Libby, the imprisoned officers have stood shivering for days in the, cold. On Christmas day it appears the Yankees went dinnerless, because there was no wood to cook their food. .A few days thereafter, the dinner tables used by the officers were consumed for fuel to cook their food with.

CHAPTER VIII

THE NEGROES IN LIBBY

There was attached to the prison about twenty "native Americans of African descent," who had been cooks and officers' servants in the Union army, but who, through the fortunes of war, had at various times been captured and brought to this popular hotel for "Yankee" soldiers. They worked in and around the prison, scrubbing floors, carrying out slops, and cutting wood.

For the most trifling offences, either imagined or real, they were stripped and tied over a tobacco hogshead or pork barrel, when Dick Turner, to gratify his devilish nature, would give the poor fellows on the bare back from thirty to forty lashes, with a horse-whip or cat-o-nine tails. The piteous moans and screams of the unoffending victims ascending from the cellar in which the brutal work was enacted, was frequently heard in the prison above. Thank God! that such scenes can never recur in the land of Washington, without the guilty perpetrators having to answer to a tribunal of justice for the crime.

The" General," one of the negroes above mentioned, was quite an original, and one of the peculiarities of Libby, never to be forgotten by the boarders at that place. It was the "General's" duty to go through the prison every morning with a kettle of burning tar, fumigating the rooms. He would inform us on each occasion that the smoke was "bery benewicial to the gemmen, kase it was good Union smoke."

THE LIBBY TUNNEL

After the enterprise contemplated by the "Council of Five" was abandoned, the leaders of that organization determined to escape from the prison by tunneling from the lower story or basement of the building, provided access could in any way be had to that part of the prison. A league, consisting of thirty-one members, each of whom was sworn not to divulge the existence of the enterprise, even to his most intimate friend, was organized to put the scheme into execution. They finally gained admittance to the cellar by carefully removing a few brick from the hearth in the lower room of the prison, and descending through the chimney flue; which was done at night, after all except those engaged in the work had retired to their respective places, to sleep and dream perchance of home and liberty.

All traces of their nocturnal labors were cleared away and closed up before the morning light. The first tunnel was commenced near the south way, with the intention of rnining through to the sewer under Canal street. This plan was found impracticable, on account of water flowing in from the sewer. Colonel Streight then proposed that an aperture be made in the stone wall under the east end of the building, and the tunnel made under the alley leading from Eighteenth street to Carey street. The proposition was at once adopted: and the work begun. The basement from whence this tunnel was commenced, was very spacious and dark, and rarely opened. and, as has been before mentioned, had the appearance of not being cleaned for years. Hence it was no trouble to conceal and dispose of the earth taken from the excavation. At the base of the east wall, and about twenty feet from the Carey street front, was the entrance to the tunnel, which was hidden when the work was not going on by a large rock which fitted the aperture exactly. Its passage lay directly beneath the tread of three sentinels, who walked the breadth of the east end of the prison, across a paved alleyway, a distance of more than fifty feet, breaking up inside of the inclosure in the rear of the building known as Carr's warehouse. So nicely was the distance gauged, that the inside of the inclosure was struck precisely at the point desired. The whole length of the tunnel was about sixty feet, with a diameter just large enough for a large sized man to pass through, though in one of the curvatures worked around a rock it was smaller; here Colonel .Streight, who by the way is somewhat inclined to corpulency, stuck fast, and was compelled to back out, and divest himself of coat, vest and shirt, when he was able to squeeze through, pulling the garments aforesaid through with a string after him.

The time consumed in digging this subterranean route to liberty was about three weeks. Several weeks, however, had been employed in fruitless efforts to make an opening in other directions, before this route was projected. The work was completed on the night of ·February the 8th, 1863, and about nine o'clock the evening of the 9th, those engaged in the enterprise commenced passing out; a knowledge of the hole then became general, and each one at once resolved to go out. The scene that followed was truly amusing and ludicrous - officers disengaging themselves from the blankets in which they had wrapped up for the night, and running hither and thither, begging, borrowing, stealing and buying a few crusts of corn bread, meat, or other edibles of whatever description they could get, anything to stay the cravings of nature for a day or two, or until they could find a friendly negro.

But of the seven hundred, or eight hundred men, that crowded, jammed and pushed around the entrance to the little avenue that led to freedom, only one hundred and nine, from nine o'clock Tuesday evening until daylight Wednesday morning, succ- eeded in getting to it and escaping.

The discovery was first made at the daily morning count, when the number of prisoners fell alarmingly short. The roll was then resorted to, as is always the case when the count does not correspond with the number booked. The calling of the roll consumed nearly four hours, and out of the one thousand and fifty odd officers confined in the prison the day previous, one hundred and nine were found to be missing. At first they suspicioned that the guards had been bribed, and connived at the escape; this suspicion we tried to strengthen, hoping that the true manner of their departure might remain a secret until another night, which would give a hundred more an opportunity of bidding our rebel hosts farewell, or rather of taking French leave without settling our board bill, or using that parting salutation.

The officer of the guard, and the sentinels on duty the night previous, were accordingly placed under arrest by Major Turner, and after being searched for money or other evidences of their criminality, confined in Castle Thunder, in order that further developments might either establish their innocence or fix their guilt upon them. In the meantime Major Turner and Lieutenant LaTouche made a thorough inspection of the basement of the prison, which slopes downwards from Carey street towards the river dock. The entrance to the tunnel was discovered, although at that time hidden by the large rock which fitted the aperture exactly. This stone rolled away from the mouth of the sepulcher, revealed the avenue which led to the outer world, and through which one hundred and odd Yankees had recently journeyed. A small negro boy was sent into the tunnel on a tour of exploration, and by the time Turner and LaTouche gained the outside of the building, a shout from the negro announced his arrival at the terminus of the subterranean route.

Couriers were early dispatched in every direction, and the pickets double posted on all the roads and bridges. Dick Turner and a posse of the prison attaches galloped off, the redoubtable Dick swearing that he would bring Streight back dead or alive; he returned, however, in a few hours without seeing Streight; and I am inclined to the opinion that it was well for him that he did not, for in all probability if he had, he would now be enjoying warmer quarters than the cell in the basement of Libby prison.

The following account of the affair is from the Richmond Dispatch. It will be seen from this that the manner of gaining admittance to the cellar was not discovered by the rebel officials. It was the impression among them for a long time, in fact until informed better by one of our own officers, that the basement was entered as stated in the following newspaper article. Fifty-five of the one hundred and nine succeeded in getting through to our lines:

"IMPORTANT ESCAPE OF YANKEE PRISONERS,
OVER FIFTY FEET OF GROUND TUNNELED

The most important escape of Federal prisoners which has occurred during the war took place at the Libby prison sometime during last Tuesday night. Of the eleven hundred Yankee officers confined therein, one hundred and nine failed to answer to their names at roll-call yesterday morn-ing. Embraced in this number were eleven Colonels, seven Majors, thirty-two Captains, and fifty-nine Lieutenants. The following is a list of the Colonels and Majors:

"Colonel A. D. Streight, of the Fifty-First Indiana regiment, a notorious character captured in Tennessee by General Forrest, and charged with having raised a negro regiment; Colonel W. G. Ely, of the Eighteenth Connecticut; Colonel J. F. Boyd, of the Twentieth army corps; Colonel H. C. Hobart, of the Twenty-First Wisconsin; Colonel W. P. Kendrick, of the Third West Tennessee cavalry; Colonel W. B. McCreary, of the Twenty-First Michigan; Colonel Thomas E. Rose, of the SeventJ7-Seventh Pennsylvania; Colonel J. P.

Spofford, of the Ninety-Seventh New York; Colonel C. W. Tilden, of the Sixteenth Maine; Colonel T. S. West, of the Twenty-Fourth Wisconsin; Colonel D. Miles, of the Nineteenth Pennsylvania; Major J. P. Collins, of the Twenty-Ninth Indiana; Major G. W. Fitzsimmons, of the Thirty-Seventh Indiana; Major J. H. Hooper, of the Fifteenth Mis$ouri; Major B. B. Macdonald, of the One Hundredth Ohio; Major A. Von Mitzel, of the Seventy-Fourth Pennsylvania.; Major I. N. Walker, of the Seventy-Third Indiana; Major J. A. Henry, of the Fifth Ohio.

    Immediately on discovering the absence of these prisoners some excitement was created among the Confederate officers in charge of the prison, and in a short time every means was adopted to ascertain the manner of their escape. At first Major Turner was inclined to the opinion that the sentinels on duty had been bribed to pass them out, and this impression was strengthened by the assertion of the Yankees remaining behind that the work had been accomplished through means of heavy fees, which had been paid a Confederate officer in the building, and his influence over the guard in their behalf. On learning this the order was given to place the guard under arrest and commit them to Castle Thunder. Not feeling satisfied about the matter, the Major and Lieutenant La Touche determined to leave no stone unturned to ferret out the mystery, and thereupon proceeded to institute a search in every direction for further information. After a fruitless examination of every part of the building where it was thought possible for a man to escape, they were about abandoning further investigation, when the idea struck them that some clue might be obtained by going into the lot on the opposite side of the street, when a large hole was soon discovered in the corner of one of the stalls of a shed which had been used as a stable, and on a line with the street running between it and the Libby prison. This discovery fully satisfied them that they had found

A Yankee in Rebel Prisons

out the means by which the escape had been made, and their next step was to trace out the spot where the tunneling was commenced. Some few yards from the eastern end of the building, in the basement, it was found tho.t a large piece of granite, about three feet by two, had been removed from the foundation, and a tunnel extending fifty-nine feet across the street, eastward, into a vacant lot formerly known as Carr's warehouse, cut through. This tunnel was about seven feet from the surface of the street, and from two and a half to three feet square. The lot in which the excavation emptied is several feet below the street, and the fleeing prisoners, when they emerged from the tunnel, found themselves on level ground. Running on Cary street is a brick building, through the center of which is a large arch, with a wooden gate to permit egress and ingress to and from the lot. By this route they got into Canal street, and keeping close to the eaves of the building .they succeeded in eluding the vigilance of the sentinels 011 duty. The prisoners are confined in the second story of the Libby prison, and the first and basement stories had to be attained before the mouth of the tunnel could be reached. From the first floor leading to the basement there was formerly a stairway, but since the building has been in use as a prison the aperture at the head of the steps has been closed with very heavy planks.

By some means the prisoners would cut through both these floors, when they wished to gain the cellar, and when they had passed down closed up the holes with the planks which had been taken out, so neatly that it could not be discovered. The cellar covers the whole area of the building, and is only used as a place for storing away meal, &c., for the use of the prison. It being very large only the front part was required, and therefore the back part of it, which is considerably below Cary street, is scarcely ever visited. The dirt which accumulated as the work progressed was spread about this part of the basement and then covered over with a large quantity of straw which has been deposited therein. It is not known how long the operatives 10 this .stupendous undertaking have been engaged; but, when the limited facilities which they possessed is taken into consideration, there can be no doubt that months have elapsed since the work was first begun. The whole thing was skillfully managed and bears the impress of master minds and indomitable perseverance.

Sometime since a Yankee Captain was found in the cellar, and on being taken before Major Turner, all smeared up with meal, be gave as his excuse for being there that he did not get enough to eat and was looking for something to make bread with. This was doubtless a falsehood, and his only business was to assist in the work which they had in hand.

There seems to be no doubt that further escape through this avenue was contemplated, and the earnestness with which the prisoners who remained behind tried to throw the blame upon the guard was only done to prevent further inquiry into the matter, and thereby leave the tunnel open for others to pass through. Probably one more night might have emptied the prison of the whole number confined therein.

Yesterday workmen were engaged in stopping up the passage which had been made from the prison, and it may now safely be relied on that no other prisoners will ever take their departure from the Libby against the knowledge and consent of the officers in charge.

As soon as the facts of the escape became fully known, orders were received by Colonel Brown, commanding the cavalry battalion for local defense, that a detachment of his force should immediately scour the surrounding country in pursuit of them, and accordingly twenty-five men from each company soon started off for that purpose: Four of the prisoners who succeeded in getting out were, late in the afternoon, recaptured and brought back. They had gotten about twenty-two miles from the city before they were over-taken. It is hardly probable, from the steps which have been taken to prevent it, that many of them will succeed in reaching the Yankee lines."

It will be seen from the above, that extraordinary efforts were made by the rebels for the recapture of the escaped Yankees, with what success has been already stated. A history of the adventures, toil and suffering of the fifty-four who reached the Union lines, would, alone, form a truly interesting volume. From the conversation I have had with several of them since I escaped myself from rebel clutches, I am able to give the following sketches of their weary pilgrimage to the land of liberty. I will first follow Colonel Streight and Captain Scearce of the Fifty-First Indiana, and Major McDonald and Lieutenant Sterling, of the One Hundredth Ohio Volunteers, on their march northward. They left Libby early in the evening, only three or four others having went through the tunnel before them. Emerging from the long, dark passage, they came up inside of the enclosure in the rear of the building, known as Carr's warehouse, from whence they passed off, singly, through an arched gateway, to Canal street, passing around the south and west sides of Libby prison, within a few feet of the sentinels on duty. As they were proceeding along Eighteenth street a man ran out of a grocery and commanded them to halt. The order not being complied with, he followed them several rods, repeating it every few yards. This gave them some uneasiness, not that they had any thought of surrendering to one man, but they feared he would keep up the chase and demands for them to halt, until the attention of other parties was attracted, and a crowd collected, when any attempt at resistance would be useless. He proved, however, to be only a drunken soldier, and had mistaken the fugitive Yankees for some of his comrades whom be wished to join. Without further incident or molestation they proceeded as according: to previous arrangement made with Mrs. Abbey Green, with whom they had been corresponding, through the agency of a colored boy who was allowed access to the prison, to the house of a negro woman, who immediately notified Mrs. Green of their arrival. That lady at once obeyed the summons, and winding through the dark and narrow alleys, was soon in close consultation with them in regard to future movements.

Leaving the negro hut, Mrs. Green directed her course to the house of Mr. Quarrelles, the absconding prisoners following in pairs within sight. The whole party finally arrived at this gentleman's residence, where they found Mrs. L. A. Rice, a lady with whom they had also been corresponding while in prison. She kindly gave up her rooms to the escaped prisoners, and made purchases of under clothing for them, also provisions for their subsistence on their journey northward; in fact, the Union people with whom they came in contact, seemed to vie with each other in their exertions for the comfort and safety of Colonel Streight and his companions.

During their stay at the house of Mr. Quarrelles they were visited by several Union men, who furnished them with money, revolvers and ammunition. Several of them also went out on pretext of hunting game, to reconnoiter the position of the rebel lines, and ascertain the most safe and practicable place to pass their pickets. One Union man visited Libby prison the morning following the escape, for the purpose of gaining what information he could in regard to the plans and extent of the preparations made for the recapture of the runaways. While there he learned that the officials

A Yankee in Rebel Prisons

connected with the prison, from General Winder down, were very lugubrious over the escape of Colonel Streight, and talked as though they would be content for all the other prisoners to get through safely, if they only could get the Colonel again in their clutches, either alive or dead. It would appear, however, from the instructions given the parties sent out for his recapture, that they preferred having him in the latter condition, as the order was to kill him if found. So anxious were the Richmond officials and the rebels of that city for the recapture or murder of Streight, that the Dispatch got up a canard that he had been killed up the James River Canal, and his body brought to the city; when this was discovered to be false, a rumor was circulated that he was still lurking about Richmond, and had been seen in a certain building on Main street; a search was immediately instituted on said premises for the Yankee Colonel, of which the following amusing account appeared in the Richmond Examiner:

"SEEING STREIGHT. - Between four and five o'clock on Tuesday afternoon, a posse of Government detectives and guards bustled into the office of Messrs. Mahoney and Hunt, dentists, on the first floor of number two hundred and eleven Main street, between ninth and tenth streets. Their spokesman, detective Craddock, after taking in sufficient breath, inquired, "I want to see Streight! " Now the officer was not cross-eyed, so Doctor Hunt replied," well, if you want to see Streight you can do so when you find him; but he is not in my keeping." The detective and his posse laughed. " Now, come, trot him out, we know he is here; for he was seen here yesterday." Doctor Hunt and his partner were getting annoyed. "Would the posse search his apartments?" That they would. So the doctor led them straightway to the business of overturning and ransacking things. They penetrated his wardrobe, spilled over his couch, looked straight up the chimney, and it is said even looked into his dentist bowl, shaving cup and bottles for the lilliputian form of whiskey Streight. They descended into the basement, reconnoitered the four corners of it, and straightway returned. Had a microscope been handy they would have looked into things a little closer. But they were not to be put off without Streight; so the whole posse took up a straight bee line for the second story. Now it so happened that it was here that Pharaoh had set up one of his tabernacles, and hard by was the secret jungle of "ye tiger." And when they that sat with Pharaoh, watching the gamboling of "ye tiger," heard of the entrance and searching below, and the feet of men upon the stairs, they said, "Truly, the Tycoon and his mandarin be upon us," and straightway broke for the roof, the coat tails of several prominent members of the lower House, whisking in mad haste to the upper House, the skylight and the roof.

" Meanwhile, the report spread that Colonel A. D. Streight and several of his officers were in the house, and that the search for them was then progressing. Hundreds of excited citizens rushed to the spot, and in five minutes the house was surrounded, front and rear. The flight of the card party seemed to confirm the report, and as the Egyptians were seen running and leaping from roof to roof, the cry arose on all sides, "here they go, there they go! there's Streight!" (gentleman in black, with hair straight on end and coat tail straight out), "shoot him, shoot him! " The situation of the people's representatives on the roof was getting straightened indeed, as they had much to fear from their excited constituents below, who now numbered at least a thousand. Several loaded muskets arrived upon the scene, followed by any number of plug ugly revolvers. Excited citizen in the rear got the range of the *impromptu* Streight and blazed away at him as he dodged between two chimneys, but the excited marksman did not see straight, or shut both eyes and did not see at all, and missed him, wounding a chimney severely. One by one the fugitives disappeared from sight, having discovered friendly traps, through which they descended, escaping a trap discretion taught them to avoid. Still the exciting Yankee hunt was continued, and the points of blood-thirsty looking weapons were elevated, turning around and searching about for a target. Doctor Mahoney venturing to examine the rear of his yard to see if it was guarded, presented his bead at the back window, when an urchin yelled, "There he is; there's Streight! " and fired at him with a pocket pistol, doing no harm, so excited and nervous was the hand that held the weapon. Finally, after the lapse of about an hour, people regained their senses in a measure, and departed in pairs to take whiskey straight in lieu of Colonel A. D. Streight.

There were several negroes in the second story when the advance on them was made by the officers, who, in stalking for the Yankee Jackal, started the Confederate tiger. One of them ran, monkey-like, across the next roof, descended a trap and fell through a skylight, a distance of thirty feet, striking upon and demolishing the baluster of a stairway in the house of Mrs. Rees. The negro was not hurt in the least, and picking himself up, scaled a rear portico and was seen no more.

"It appears, from what we have since learned, that the search was made upon the strength of information communicated to Colonel Rees, of the President's staff, in an anonymous letter. The letter stated that Colonel Streight had been seen there the previous day. We suspect that the whole affair was a plot to reveal the existence of a violation of the gaming law, as carried on in the second story, over Messrs. Mahoney and Hunt's office, and with which they have nothing to do. About seven o'clock the same evening there was another excitement at the same place, in consequence of men being seen passing rapidly from one roof to another on a ladder thrown across. It was Streight again, .making his exit from his hiding place, and straightway there was another hubbub.

The whole story of Streight's presence in Richmond may be set down as a straight-out-and-out "sell" of very huge calibre.

At the same time this exciting hunt for Streight was going on, he and his whole party were lying concealed as before mentioned, and had the satisfaction of reading the above account the next morning after it transpired, also the *Dispatch's* account of the Colonel's murder up the canal. They remained at the house of Mr. Quarrelles one week, recruiting strength for the long and dangerous journey before them. At nine o'clock in the evening of the eighth day of their stay in Richmond, accompanied by a guide, and two deserters from Camp Lee, well armed and provided with provisions, they started out on the long weary march northward; after passing outside the works and fortifications, unseen by the troops on duty there, they directed their course by a small pocket compass about fifteen degrees east of north, and the same night crossed the Chickahominy river within full view of the rebel pickets. Here one of the deserters who had started with the party from Richmond became frightened and left, causing some anxiety in the minds of the fugitives, lest he should betray them to the troops doing duty along the course of the river. The second night out the whole party suffered severely, the weather being extremely cold, and they thinly clad and without blankets, and dare not build fires, which might attract attention and be the means of leading to their recapture. They traveled next night, avoiding all roads, but the whole party was already so much fatigued and their legs and feet so much swollen, that they were able to make only a few miles in the direction of the happy land they were seeking. The next day was so intensely cold, that fatigued and worn out as they were, they were obliged to keep moving to prevent perishing. During this day's march, they arrived on the south bank of the Pamunkey river, which they found flowing with great huge cakes of ice that jammed and crushed each other, producing a noise like the roar of a dozen Niagaras; to cross this stream was of the utmost importance for the present safety of the fugitives. But how was this to be accomplished? There was no boat at hand, or any place in the vicinity that one could be procured, and even if they had a boat it seemed like madness to attempt pushing it through the surging waters, and between the vast acres of ice floating with the current, sweeping every thing before it. To delay was hazarding their liberty, to push forward seemed certain destruction; they were brave and determined men, and the situation made them desperate; they, therefore, resolved on building a raft of rails, poles and bark, and trust their fate to the angry element in preference to the ferocious dogs and savage men in pursuit. The raft completed, all got aboard, and soon the frail craft, in obedience to the propelling power of its cargo of human freight, was dodging through the crevices, and into the open spaces formed by the cracking and splits in the ice fields. After an hour of peril and incessant labor, the north bank of the stream was safely reached, and with a shout of triumph and gladness the whole party stepped on shore. But before the top of the bank was gained, they were discovered by a squad of rebel scouts. Was it possible they had periled their lives crossing the fearful stream to fall immediately in the hands of the enemy, and be again consigned to the horrid dungeons and cells of the Richmond prisons? No, fortune favored them; the rebel soldiery, winding through the swamp and tangled brush and cedars, lost sight of them, of which they took advantage and securely concealed themselves in a dense pine thicket, where they remained undisturbed until after nightfall, when they again started on their weary pilgrimage, avoiding as usual all public roads. This night's march brought them to the Mattaponi river, which, like the Pumunkey, was running full of ice, but they fortunately found a very good boat, and crossed with but little difficulty; and soon afterwards gray streaks of' light began making their appearance in the east, warning the fugitives that their safety demanded they should select a place of , concealment until the dark shades of night again enveloped the earth. After a suitable place was secured, a small fire was built to heat the sand, in which they would bury their feet during the day to keep them from freezing. They dare not risk building a fire after sunrise, lest the smoke should attract attention and lead to their discovery and recapture.

    The fifth night out, they traveled over an extremely rough country, through tangled brush and briers. In the latter part of the night they met a negro, from whom they learned that they were in the vicinity of Rappahannock Station; and from the information gained from him, they concluded it was best to bivouac in a swamp about two miles from the village. The ice was running in large quantities in the Rappahannock river, making a rumbling noise that could be heard for miles. The weather was still very cold, consequently in their thinly clad condition they suffered extremely with the frost; their stock of provisions was also about exhausted, but a negro fortunately discovered them in their hiding place, and conducted them to his hut, and gave them an abundant supply of corn bread and bacon. The next morning they were discovered and pursued by soldiers, citizens and hounds; they pushed on, however, and when the dogs came up they fed and urged them on, as though they were not the party whose trail they were scenting. During the day two of the party gave out from over exertion and loss of sleep, and had to be supported by the others in order to get along. They were surrounded by the rebels in pursuit three times, but by concealing themselves in the laurel thickets, and frequently changing their location, they were able to hold out until night, when they felt quite safe, although surrounded on the east, north and west by water, and on the south by a chain of rebel pickets, which left them in a space, the area of which did not exceed two miles in width and five miles in length, with about six hundred soldiers and a large number of citizens, with several packs of hounds on their track.

That night they went to a plantation, and was hid by the negroes in one of their huts, while the darkies themselves went with their masters to join in the hunt for the runaway Yankee officers. The negroes found a boat of at least forty tons burthen, anchored on the opposite side of a stream about two hundred yards wide, which empties in the Rappahannock river. About ten o'clock, P. M., they started for the vessel, accompanied by the negroes; arriving at the stream, a raft was quickly constructed and pushed out towards the boat, which was soon reached, and all got aboard, including the negroes, who assisted to row the vessel down the bayou to the river, and then returned to the plantation. The Rappahannock, which at this point is three miles wide, was crossed without difficulty, and the boat then turned adrift. The following day they rested in the pine thickets as usual, and at night started out, marching in great pain through woods, swamps, and over hills, arriving about daylight on the bank of the Potomac river, opposite Blackstone's Island, when they met a negro who directed them to the house of a Union man, (a German,) who was the owner of a boat; with him they remained until night, when they went to the river to cross, the German and two or three of his friends at the same time going up to the bayou where the vessel was moored to bring it into the river. While on this mission they were discovered by a squad of rebel soldiers, (about twenty,) who, supposing it was Colonel Streight and his party, opened fire on them, wounding one and capturing the others. But our Yankee friends, unobserved, "retreated in good order," where they secreted themselves, occasionally "changing their base," until the next night, when they went back to the house of their German friend, from whom they learned that the rebel soldiery had mistaken him, and the men with him, for escaped prisoners. They remained at this place for two days, waiting for an opportunity to cross the Potomac river, which at this point is eight miles wide; while here they were in full view of a part of the Potomac flotilla, which they repeatedly signaled with a white shirt, but no notice was taken of it by any of the vessels.

The German finally succeeded in getting a boat from a friend some miles further up the river. They then set sail for Blackstone's Island, and arrived there at two o'clock, A. M., the twenty-eighth day of February, and were kindly received at the house of Dr. Williams. The next day they took passage with acting Commodore Parker, of the Potomac squadron, and arrived in Washington the first of March.

A long, weary, and perilous pilgrimage had been theirs. Eleven days and nights of watching and anxiety, of cold and hunger, of peril and hairbreadth escapes, of threading thickets and marshes, of crossing streams, and shelterless sleeping on the ground, of lacerated feet and frost bitten hands, of alternating hope and despair, was their varied and bitter experiences. But it was liberty they sought, and they gained it. Bravery, energy, perseverance, the kindly moon and polar star, and the negro guide, brought them safe within our lines. Freedom, friends, and the protecting folds of the stars and stripes, was their reward.

CHAPTER IX

KILPATRICK'S ATTEMPT TO RELEASE THE PRISONER

Demonstrations on the rebel Capital by the Union cavalry, during our sojourn there, were of frequent occurrence, but generally resulted in nothing more than giving Jeff Davis and the rebel office-ials a "big scare," and carrying off a few negroes, The last of these movements was the famous raid of General Kilpatrick in February, when the brave and lamented Dahlgren yielded up his gallant young life a noble sacrifice on the altar of his country - the bullet of a cowardly and concealed foe mortally wounding him while with his command protecting the rear of Kilpatrick's retreating column.

In the earlier stages of the war, reports were in circulation to the effect that the rebel soldiery carried from the bloody field of Manassas the bones of our gallant dead, and afterwards manufact-ured them into rings and ornaments which they sent home as troph-ies to their female friends, who, wearing them, would point to the ring on the finger, or the cross swinging from the neck, and with savage pride boast that the one was made from a Yankee's skull, and the other from the bones of his limbs. These stories, although extensively circulated, received but little credit. Our people could not realize the possibility of civilized men and women sinking to a depth of barbarism that would prompt such inhuman and malicious outrages on the bodies of their dead fellow beings. But these acts, even if true, were human and Christian when compared with the fiendish mutilation and disposition of the body of the murdered Dahlgren. What this was, we only know from their own statements, and give the following account of it from the Richmond Examiner:

"Dahlgren's body was boxed up at Walkerton on Sunday and brought to Richmond, with the object, we understand, of its positive identification, and the establishment of the fact of the finding of the infamous documents upon it, all of which has been attested by witnesses. Henceforth the name of Dahlgren is linked 'with eternal infamy, and in the years to come defenseless woman and innocent childhood will peruse, with a sense of shrinking horror, the story of Richmond's rescue from the midnight sack and ravage led by Dahlgren. It would seem something of the curse he came to bestow upon others lighted upon his own carcass, when it fell riddled by avenging Southern bullets. Stripped, robbed of every valuable, the fingers cut off for the sake of the diamond rings that encircled them, when the body was found by those sent to take charge of it, it was lying in a field stark naked, with the exception of the stockings. Some humane persons had lifted the corpse from the pike and thrown it over into the field, to save it from the hogs. The artificial leg worn by Dahlgren was removed, and is now at General Elzey's headquarters. It is of most beautiful design and finish.

Yesterday afternoon the body was removed from the car that brought it to the York River railroad depot, and given to the spot of earth selected to receive it. Where that spot is no one but those concerned in its burial know or care to tell. It was a dog's burial, without coffin, winding sheet or service. Friends and relatives at the North need inquire no further; this is all they will know - he is buried a burial that befitted the mission upon which he came. He has "swept through the city of Richmond'" on a pine bier, and "written his name" on the scroll of infamy, instead of "on the hearts of his countrymen," never to be erased. He "asked the blessing of Almighty God" on his mission of rapine, murder and blood, and the Almighty cursed him instead."

Copies of the orders issued by Colonel Dahlgren to his troops were found upon his person. What purported to be *verbatim* copies of these orders were published in the Richmond papers, but

A Yankee in Rebel Prisons

they were too ridiculous and absurd to be credited by any except misguided and blinded rebels, as the addresses of a commanding officer to his troops. According to these neither age nor sex was to be spared, nor mercy nor quarter shown - all was to be put to the sword.

This expedition of Kilpatrick's, although a portion of his troops came in sight of the rebel Capital – in fact inside of the outer works protecting that stronghold of treason - from some cause proved a most lamentable and disastrous failure.

PLOT TO BLOW UP THE PRISON.

We now come to a chapter in the history of the infamous rebellion just conquered by the armies of the Union, which, in its wicked design and malignity, surpasses any act of cruelty on the black records of crime. Kilpatrick's force was greatly overestimated by the rebel officials in Richmond; the design of the expedition was also somewhat shrouded in mystery. It was supposed by them, however, that it contemplated the release of the Union prisoners of war confined .there. At this time there were but a few regular troops in the defenses of the city, consequently they did not feel very sanguine of their ability to hold the place against a. sudden dash of cavalry. But they resolved that, under no circumstances, should the officers and prisoners of war confined in Libby be returned to their friends and the defense of their country by being released with force of arms; .and a project for our destruction that would shock even the cruel nature of a Nena Sahib was planned, and ready to be executed the moment the Union forces entered the city.

An excavation was made in the cellar of the prison in which was placed several hundred pounds of powder, and a fuse attached ready to ignite and blow the building, inmates, and all to atoms, in case they were unable to repulse Kilpatrick.

The evidence of the existence of this scheme to destroy the prisoners by blowing up the building with gunpowder was abundant, and the source from whence it came such that its truth could not be questioned. The operation of placing the powder there was seen by our men confined in the cell, and by the negroes quartered in that part of the prison, who were afterwards removed to another apartment and warned to keep away from their old place. The Richmond Sentinel, referring to the matter, said such measures had been adopted by the prison officials that the Yankee officers would never be released by Federal troops. Dick Turner himself remarked to one of our officers that if Kilpatrick had succeeded in getting into the city, Libby and every d - d Yankee in it would have been blown to h - ll before they should have been released.

It is well for the city of Richmond that this horrible plot was not executed, as no power on earth could have restrained the desire of the Union soldier for vengeance, and today there would only be a huge pile of brick and stone - smouldering ruins of the Confederate capital to mark the place where the treasonable city once stood.

REMOVAL FROM LIBBY

'Tis May sixth, 1864; eight days more and we will have been here *one year,* a year of torturing anxiety, conflicting hopes and fears; a year of suffering, deprivation and inhuman treatment; a year lost ·to ourselves, to our country and our friends, except, perhaps, we have acquired in a greater degree the virtue of patience and the ability to meet, with fortitude and resignation, the fate that the fortunes of war have imposed upon us.

May sixth - a day long to be remembered in the history of our country has passed with the usual dull, monotonous routine of duties, occupations and amusements, and the sombre shades of night again envelop Libby and its inmates, nearly all of whom have sought their respective places on the floor and earnestly court sleep, that blissful relief for the weary, suffering and heart-sore prisoner. But ere Morpheus established his supremacy through the apartments of Libby, we were startled by an order from the prison commandant to be ready to march at one o'clock the next morning. Disorder and confusion followed this order; everyone was instantly busily engaged " packing up" with the intention of taking with him the few articles of comfort he had remaining of what had been sent from home, but an order comes from the authorities that we will not be allowed to take anything with us more than we are able to carry to Petersburg, to which point it is announced we will have to march. But where are they going to take us? is the question anxiously passed from one to another. Some over-sanguine individual who, perhaps, has been but a short time a resident of Libby, feels quite certain that we are going to be exchanged, as he had some time previous heard Major Turner say that the exchange would be almost certain to come when no one was expecting it. It was also argued by some that the authorities would not send us off unless it was for exchange, without allowing us to take with us those articles we had received from friends in the North. Verily those uninitiated "fresh fish" have since had good cause for changing their opinion of the consideration and regard rebel officials had for the feelings and comfort of Yankee prisoners ·of war. Very few, however, took stock in exchange, but all were glad to bid farewell to Libby, even though it was to enter another prison.

It is true we had heard of the terrible ravages of disease among our soldiers confined in the pest-houses at Danville, and of the horrors of the Andersonville prison pen. But to those of us who had endured for a dozen long months the deprivations of Libby life - never, for a moment, walking abroad into the outer world, and never breathing for once the pure air of heaven – any change was desirable.

At one o'clock on the morning of the seventh, they commenced counting us *out* of Libby; this operation consumed the time until daylight, as each one was required to answer to his name as he passed out. As we lay in Carey street in front of the accursed building within whose hated walls we had been confined for so long a time, although still surrounded by rebel bayonets, we felt that we were free; we once more breathed the fresh, pure air, and the beams of the morning sun again shone on us, what a happy transition, it almost made us feel that we were going home, to liberty and the defense of our country. But we were still in the hands of the enemy, and many months of suffering, cold, hunger and semi-starvation was yet in store for us. And many of our number, alas! were going to the far off South never to return, and their bones now moulder around the prison hells at Salsbury, Andersonville, Macon, Millen, Charleston and Columbia.

When we bid good by to Libby, we rejoiced that we were out of the hands of those fiendish monsters in human shape, General Winder, Major Turner, commandant of the prison, and Dick Turner, inspector of the same.

Soon after daylight our motley crowd of half nude men was marched to the Danville depot to take the cars for that place. The story that we would have to march to Petersburg being a rebel lie, for the purpose of compelling us to leave in the Libby prison the large amount of sugar, coffee, tea, &c., that we had on hand, and which had been sent us from home. When we left Libby we were placed under charge of Captain Tabb, of whom more anon.

Arriving at Danville we were crowded into two frame buildings, where we were confined in less than half the space we had *enjoyed* in Libby. In fact No. 3 prison, in which I was confined, the whole Space allotted us was completely covered at night when all were stretched out on the floor to sleep, and even in this crowded condition we were not allowed a breeze of fresh air, the narrow windows being tightly boarded up two-thirds of the way from bottom to top, consequently the high temperature and impurity of the air was such that we almost suffocated. One evening, during our stay there, the oppressive heat and fetid air became so intolerable that one of the prisoners attempted to knock off one of the boards nailed over one of the windows, and was shot at by the rebel guard on the outside of the building.

We remained at Danville only five days - about the same length of time that Jeff Davis and the heads of the departments of the rebel government sojourned there nearly one year afterwards, when fleeing from Richmond with the Confederate capital in a carpetbag.

Before leaving Danville we were furnished by the rebel commissary with one pound and a half of cornbread and one-half pound of bacon, and this is all we received until we arrived at Augusta, Georgia, three days afterwards, consequently those who had to depend on the rebels for subsistence during the time (and this was nearly all) were absolutely in a famishing condition; yet, notwithstanding this, we were not permitted to purchase provisions of the numerous peddlers and hucksters who crowded around the train at the depots and stations at which we stopped along the route.

At Augusta we discovered that Macon was our intended destination. Up to this time we had no idea where we were going, though there were many rumors current in regard to this all important matter. One would say that he had it from good authority that we were going to Savannah to be exchanged, while another would report that he had it from the same source that Texas would be our journey's end."

Arrived at Macon May Seventeenth, 1864, one year and one day from the time we entered Libby - a years' imprisonment. We could scarcely realize the fact that so many of us still survived the hardships and suffering of those dozen lonely, cheerless months, and when we remembered the friends whom we had seen carried out to their final resting places during that time, we could not repress a fearful shudder in contemplation of the fate awaiting ourselves. .

Crowds of citizens and soldiers, full of eager curiosity were soon collected around the cars to get a glimpse of the *distinguished arrivals.* From them we learned that the "Old Fair Grounds, a delightful place," had been put in order for our reception. This was glorious news. Was it possible that we were no longer to be encompassed by brick walls and iron grates? that we were soon to have the privilege of breathing the pure air, and enjoying the bright sunshine?

Two long lines of guards are formed on one side of the train, we are then counted out of the cars and in between these lines of sentinels. Soon as all are off the train, we are ordered forward. We are well pleased with the description given of our prospective home for the next - we dare not say how many months, for the very contemplation sends a thrill of terror through the frame, and sickens the heart - perhaps another year; each one thinks, probably, *his* home only for a few days or weeks, for many of his comrades have sickened and died, and it may be his time next.

We tramp along the dusty street around by the Government machine shops and foundry, in the vicinity of which was located the "Macon Stockade," a huge roofless pen, containing about three acres, made of boards sixteen feet in length, nailed perpendicular and close together to a railing supported by posts set in the ground. Outside of this was a plank walk, upon which the sentinels were posted every ten feet, and on the east and south sides were two large platforms, upon which cannon were mounted. Inside about fifteen feet from the outer enclosure, was a picket fence, called the "dead line," which prisoners were not allowed to approach or touch under penalty of being shot.

We had complimented ourselves that we had got out of the hands of Major Turner, and that other villain of the same name, christened Richard, now "chewing the cud of sweet and bitter fancies" in the cell in which he had delighted to starve and torture so many unfortunate prisoners of war, while in authority at Libby Prison. But we soon found out that we had gained but little by the change, for Captain Tabb, Commandant of the Macon prison, was possessed of an equally cruel, vindictive and arbitrary nature as the Turners, or Lieutenant La Touche, without the intelligence or executive ability of either, and was besides a drunkard and thief.

The prisoners sometimes bartered with the rebel guards, exchanging watches, finger-rings, knives, and other valuables for Confederate money, with which we could buy a few articles at exorbitant prices from the sutlers. Captain Tabb, by some means, learned of these transactions with the guards, and issued an order to the effect that any prisoner talking to or tampering in any manner with the guard, would be severely punished also, that if we had anything to dispose of, he would take it out and sell it for us, at the price put on it by the owner, or otherwise return it. One of the prisoners gave him a watch and chain to sell for four hundred dollars, charging him particularly not to dispose of it for less. After a few weeks had elapsed he was questioned as to the matter, when he replied that he had sold them for two hundred dollars. The officer noticed that he was wearing the chain himself, and interrogated him as to how he came by it, to which he made answer that the purchaser gave it to him. The officer then demanded of Tabb the return of his property, or the amount in money that he had ordered him to sell it for, at the same time threatening an exposition of the affair unless the demand was complied with. Upon which Captain Tabb took him out, and after abusing him with the most shameful and insulting epithets, had him "bucked" for three hours. The articles were finally restored.

The rations issued us in this prison were slightly better than we had been before receiving. Instead of the hard corn bread we got in Libby, and which Lieutenant Pavey wrote to one of his friends in the naval service would make excellent gunboat plating, we received a pint of corn meal per day, which, with a little salt and soda that we could purchase, we could make quite palatable, in fact it was really astonishing to see the variety of dishes manufactured from corn meal; among them we might mention corn-pone, corn cakes, corn fritters, corn-meal duff, corn-meal pudding, corn coffee and corn dumplings. We also received about two ounces per day of rancid bacon, which, for the want of salt, had been packed in wood ashes. Our rations were occasionally changed, when in lieu of the above articles, we got a little rice and a few " nigger peas," each of which was the habitation of one or more animate beings.

Our facilities ·for cooking and washing were not very extensive. The following were given to each squad of one hundred men: eight skillets with covers, four camp kettles, thirteen wash-pans and four wooden buckets.

A Yankee in Rebel Prisons

Cooking out of doors in the hot sun, the rain, or the wind and dust, is not very conducive to amiability, and under these circumstances many churlish husbands have vowed never again to find fault with their better half, when the roast was a little over-done, or the biscuit like themselves, somewhat sad.

A UNION OFFICER MURDERED

Just at dark of the evening of June seventeenth, an officer belonging to the Forty-fifth New York Volunteers, returning from the spring where he had been for a pail of water, was shot by one of the guards on duty at that part of the prison. He was carried up to his quarters and every aid and assistance rendered him that was in our limited power to give, but the poor fellow died before midnight. .There were several prisoners near by and standing around him when shot, but none of them could assign any reason for the act but the intention to commit a willful murder.

The senior officer in prison wrote to Captain Gibbs, who was then in command, having some days previous relieved the unprincipled Tabb, desiring that the circumstances connected with the affair be investigated. The communication was returned, with the following insulting indorsement: "Such investigation as may by me be deemed proper, will be made in this case." A few days after we learned that the guilty homicide had been promoted to be a Sergeant, and given thirty days furlough. It was generally understood that rewards of this kind were constantly held out to the sentinels on duty for like service.

It is surprising to witness the ingenuity and tact a prisoner will bring into requisition to effect an escape, and the industry and patient toil and perseverance he will display to accomplish that object. Both at Macon and Columbia two or three of the prisoners blacked themselves and passed out as negro workmen. At Macon one bribed the negro driver of the Sutler's wagon, and was taken out in a box, while another secured himself to the coupling pole and hounds of the same wagon and was hauled out in that manner, finally getting through to our lines. Others with more patience and perseverance, but less tact and daring, tried tunneling, and at least a half-dozen of these subterraneous passages were under operation at the same time. The mouth of the tunnel was in some one of the sheds or shanties occupied by a portion of the prisoners, usually under their beds; in one or two instances they were started from the place where fires were built in the day time for our culinary labors, so that when the Inspector passed through the prison, a blazing fire, with pots and kettles hanging over it, in which were being cooked our rice or black worm-eaten beans, concealed the entrance to the tunnel.

But here, as in Libby, we had traitors in our midst, men wearing the uniform of the United States army, who for a less reward than Judas received for betraying his Lord and Master, divulged to the rebel authorities the plans and schemes of their fellow-prisoners to escape from the jaws of death. On the strength of the information thus obtained, a search was instituted by the Commandant of the prison, which unmasked our work and dashed the fond hopes we had indulged in for weeks of home and liberty, to the earth.

CHAPTER X

REMOVAL FROM MACON

Toward the latter part of July General Sherman made his famous cavalry raid into the interior of Georgia, passing around Atlanta and striking the railroads east of Macon. Some days previous, in consequence of the rapid advance of Sherman on Atlanta, and the probability that he would soon occupy that city, which would render Macon untenable, the rebel authorities commenced moving the prisoners to Charleston. Two trains, loaded, had already gone to that place, and the remaining prisoners, (about three hundred,) were aboard the cars at the Macon depot the morning Stoneman's advance came in the vicinity of the city. We had been marched out from the prison at one o'clock A. M., so as to be ready for the train to leave at daylight, an event which we were all anxiously and impatiently awaiting, for nothing is so irksome and annoying as to be lying still on a railroad train, especially when one is along with sixty or seventy companions, squeezed into a stock car without seats, and with scarcely room to stand, as was the case with us. From the guards we learned that Stoneman was heading for the Savannah road, the route over which we would pass, which made us doubly anxious to be off; and while eagerly listening for the sound of the steam whistle, the signal for our departure, we were greeted with a noise of a different kind, but to us still more welcome. It was the report of artillery and musketry in the hands of Union soldiers; joy thrilled the heart of every prisoner. Our friends had heard the starving wail from Southern prisons, and had come to the rescue - happy day ! How we complimented ourselves that it bad been our fortune to remain at this place, while our comrades had been sent to a more secure locality. These were our first selfish thoughts, but when we remembered their brave, patient suffering through many lonely, weary months of deprivations, involuntary tears would start, that they were not with us to enjoy the restoration to freedom, home and friends, which we regarded as at hand. We soon hear the report of firearms more distinct and clear - it is from the guns of the rebel soldiers, who have gone out to meet and dispute the entrance of our men to the city. A few shells come whizzing through the air and land in the suburbs of the town; the noise of the conflict becomes louder and clearer, by which we know that the rebels are falling back on their works; and we feel sanguine that ere the set of sun Union soldiers will have possession of the town, and rebels will occupy our old quarters in the stockade.

While the fight is going on we are taken back and turned again inside of the prison pen, which, a few hours before, we thought we were leaving forever. This, however, did not disconcert us in the least, for we still felt confident that Stoneman's force would release us. We could yet hear the sharp crack of musketry and booming cannon which, to us, was music sweet as the voice of a beloved wife or affectionate mother. It encouraged us to hope for deliverance from a life of misery. we were still cheered by the clang of arms until about two o'clock P. M., when the sound began to grow more distant and faint, and finally died away till all was quiet as the still morning air which it had first broken, and with it *died all hope.*

Early next morning many exciting rumors were brought into the prison by rebel officers and guards concerning the fight of the previous day, and the fate of General Stoneman and his command, some saying that the whole force, except Stoneman and his body-guard had been captured; while others affirmed that Stoneman was also a prisoner; and, although we made due allowance for the usual rebel exaggerations of such matters, the news had a truly depressing influence on the spirits of the prisoners, as our knowledge of the fact that he was unable to enter the city, was evidence that he had a large force to contend against. On the thirty-first of July, being surrounded on all sides by an overwhelming force of General Wheeler's cavalry, General Stoneman was compelled to surrender, and the day following he and about fifty of his officers were consigned to the Macon prison. The undertaking to release us was a failure, and the brave officers and men of General Stoneman's command lost, in the attempt, their own liberties, instead of restoring freedom to us. On the sixteenth of August all the prisoners then remaining in Macon; were started for Charleston, packed in box cars, sixty officers and five guards in each, on the route we suffered extremely from intense heat and intolerable thirst, yet we were not allowed to open but one side of the car, nor leave the train, even with a guard, to procure a drink of water:

The first lot of prisoners that left Macon for Charleston, previous to starting, organized a secret society, with initiation oaths, pass-words, signs and grips, similar to the "Council of Five," which, it will be recollected, existed in Libby prison; the members were divided into companies and squads, to each of which was appointed a head or chief. Everything was in readiness for an outbreak whenever an opportunity offered for escape.

When the prisoners first learned the intention of the authorities to send us to Charleston, it was decided by the members of this society, that the removal would offer a favorable time for carrying their plans into execution. At a preconcerted signal to be given at some way-station, the guards inside and outside the cars, were to be seized, and their arms and ammunition secured. This would have been a very easy matter, for most of them were Georgia militia, many of whom would not even have made a show of resistance. The train, in event of success, was to have been stopped near Pocotaligo bridge, from which General Foster's lines might easily have been reached, being then only ten or twelve miles distant. Why the plan was not executed has never been fully explained. All the details of the arrangement were perfected, most of the arms of the guards were either in possession of the prisoners, or the caps removed from the tubes, and the cartridges from the boxes, so that but feeble resistance, if any, would have been offered; in fact, it is believed the whole design could have been consummated without the loss of a drop of blood.

It is alleged that it was through the cowardice of the officer chief in command of the organization, that the signal for action was not given.

We arrived at Charleston on the evening of August eighteenth; here, more than in any other city of the South, wore the signs of the desolation of war. It was, indeed, a sad sight to behold the melancholy change that the misguided people of the South, by their own wicked acts, had brought on their once great commercial metropolis. Whole rows of buildings, once the finest stores and most prosperous portions of the town, were but sad evidences of ruin, their mouldering and decaying walls tumbling piecemeal with the revolution of each successive day. Business, in fact, had scarcely a name, while former sumptuous life and social living was transformed into a miserable misanthropic existence. Hotels were deserted, and the side-walks and promenades, usurped once by fashionable belles and beaus, were but pathways for a preponderating crowd of filthy-looking negroes. Elegant ladies, rolling in luxury and wealth, who once wore silks and satins, were costumed in calicoes and muslins. Fashion, as regards dress, had deserted her throne, giving place to the sway of old styles and antiquated, seedy garments. Cheerfulness is no longer a characteristic of Southern society. The crime of which these people are guilty, is one of the greatest known to the laws of our country; but their punishment has certainly been already in proportion.

A Yankee in Rebel Prisons

The lot of prisoners of whom I was with, were first assigned quarters in the work-house, Do large massive brick-building, with heavy iron-grated doors and windows. Until the roof was riddled with shells from our mortars on James' Island, the building was the hapless reservoir of all the unmanageable negroes in the city of Charleston and vicinity, for whose accommodation that portion of it above ground was partitioned off with heavy iron and timbers into cells, and that below into dungeons. In the rear of the work-house is a yard which we were allowed the privilege of entering during the day, but the filth and stench was so intolerable that most of us preferred remaining inside the gloomy walls of brick and mortar, when not compelled to enter it to attend to our culinary affairs.

We remained here about two weeks, when we were transferred to the jail-yard, where we were associated with the scum and vilest characters of rebeldom - deserters from both the Union and rebel armies, condemned criminals, thieves, assassins and prostitutes, both black and white.

While at Macon, a few cooking utensils were furnished us, but when we left there they were all taken away. One of our officeers, for an attempt to smuggle a mess pan through, was brutally punished. And as nothing of the kind was allowed us while at Charleston, we were, consequently, without the necessary vessels in which to prepare the limited quantity of coarse food furnished us; corn-meal was issued to us all the time there, in fact, during the whole of the winter following, but no stoves, skillets, or anything of the kind in which to bake it. In the Charleston jail were heavy cast-iron spittoons; some of the prisoners bought these from the turnkey, and converted them into Dutch ovens, using pieces of old tin, which we bought of the guards, for lids or covers. I recollect the first *pone* "our mess" baked in this way, seemed to be the most palatable bread I ever tasted. Three weeks' diet on a scant allowance of boiled rice and mush, both without salt, gave us a good appetite for corn-dodgers.

At Charleston about six hundred of our officers were confined, though on parole, in the Marine and Roper hospitals. They enjoyed better accommodations, and, perhaps, received a little better rations than we who remained in the work-house and jail, as the rebel officials informed us they received these favors on account of having given their parole not to attempt escape.

The most gloomy days of my prison life were passed in this traitorous city, and the only occasions on which I could ever discover a ray of pleasure beaming from the countenances of my fellow-prisoners, was at night, when crowds of them would be collected around, the narrow-grated windows, looking far away towards the sea, watching the flashes from the mouth of the "Swamp Angel," and following, with the eye, by its tail of fire, (the burning fuse) away up among the stars, the beautiful curve of the destructive missile it hurled in the bosom of the wicked and treasonable city. Or, when the exploding shells from grim old Wagner ignited some combustible matter, and communicated the fire to the surrounding buildings, when, between the fright and consternation of the negro firemen, who were thus unable to check its progress, and our prayers for the flames to "spread from house to house," there would only remain, of the entire square in which the conflagration broke out, the black and charred brick walls, and ponderous heaps of smouldering ruins. These were pleasurable moments - happy sights! Like Nero, when Rome was in flames, we could have danced and fiddled, if the accursed city, from center to circumference, had been engulphed in the fiery element.

In the latter part of September the yellow fever made its appearance among the prisoners. Several of my most intimate friends fell victims to this terrible scourge, and it was not until death had marked them for his, that , we could induce the rebel surgeons to remove them from the dark, dank, illy-ventilated cells of the workhouse to the hospital for medical treatment. Unfortunate sufferers! noble friends! they died martyred victims on the altar of freedom, and their last resting places on the banks of the Ashley river remains unmarked by slab or stone.

As a sanitary measure, considered necessary for the general health of the city, the authorities decided to remove us to Columbia, the State capital of South Carolina. And, on the third day of October, we were ordered to get ready for the trip, but without sufficient time being allowed to prepare the necessary food for the journey, we were hurried off to the depot, and packed, as usual, sixty or seventy into a box car. Before daylight next morning we arrived in Columbia, and were corralled during the day in a vacant lot adjoining the depot. Here, sick and well alike, were exposed to the scorching rays of the burning sun, until about five o'clock in the evening, when sun and sky became obscured by terrific black clouds that poured down incessantly for nearly six hours tremendous torrents of rain, and many, coatless, hatless, shoeless and without blankets, lay all that dreary, stormy night on the cold, bare earth - bare, only where it was covered with water, which was the case with nearly the entire space assigned us for quarters. No rations had yet been issued us since leaving Charleston; it is true most of the prisoners still had a portion of the corn-meal drawn the last issue, at that place, but had no utensils or fuel with which to prepare it for eating. Had it not been for the few pies and cakes and diminutive loaves of bread brought in and sold at exorbitant prices by boys, old women, hucksters and peddlers of all descriptions, our suffering from hunger would have been .much greater. Notwithstanding the unreasonable rates at which these articles were sold, it was extremely difficult for the feeble and weaker portion of our community to get a share, even though they had plenty of money. Starving men, no matter how much benevolence or kind a heart they may possess, will seldom divide their scanty mite with others. Lieutenant Clark, of a New York regiment, in a vain attempt to purchase a corn-pone from a negro woman, who was standing near the guard with her merchandise, was mercilessly pierced in the back with a bayonet, in the hands of one of the sentinels, whose only excuse for the cruel and heartless act, was, that the Lieutenant was *nearer* his beat than the prisoners ought to go.

About ten o'clock the next morning after our thorough drenching, we were marched out three miles south of the city, and turned into a lot of nearly six acres in extent. Here, if tents or shelter of any kind had been furnished us, we would have had quite a comfortable location, as the camp was on high ground, and the water, from the heavy rains peculiar to the latitude of South Carolina during the winter months, run off freely, leaving our quarters comparatively dry; besides, we had an abundance of fresh air, a luxury not enjoyed in any of the rebel prisons in which we had been previously confined. But, if we had this advantage here, there were other inconveniences (besides miserable quarters and scant fare which were characteristic of all Confederate prisons) that quite counterbalanced it; for instance, there was neither wood nor water to be had in camp, and only six were permitted to go out at a time for either, and the same rule applied to attending the calls of nature; and opposite the gate where we were allowed to pass out for these purposes, I have frequently seen as many as one hundred and fifty men standing, anxiously awaiting their turn.

This arrangement lasted for nearly one month, when the guard-line was extended a few hours each day, so as to take in the wood and water; the latter we procured from a brook that run within about four hundred yards of our quarters. At first we had to pick up all the wood we used, but after some weeks a few hatchets and axes were furnished, when, besides getting wood for fuel, those that knew how and were able to use them, went to work building cabins or shanties out of pine poles, which they carried sometimes a mile on their backs into camp. Very few, however, could boast of the luxury of a pine cabin. The most general style of architecture was to make an excavation in the ground two or three feet deep, and as large in diameter as the enterprise or material of the builder would allow. This hole was then covered with poles, sticks and brush set on their ends, on two sides, and coming together over the center. The clay taken from the excavation was then thrown on top of these. They did not always keep the rain out, but, under the circumstances, were considered quite comfortable. There were a few structures of this kind of more aristocratic pretensions, and could boast the luxury of a chimney and fire-place, all, of course, built of clay.

    Others, who could not procure the use of either axe, hatchet or spade, constructed temporary screens from wind and frost, by making a lattice-work of vines and twigs, and thatching it with pine boughs; in fact, the various styles of cabins, shanties, huts and caves, constructed here by our own hands, and almost without the use of tools of any kind, were nearly as numerous and diversified as the habits and opinions of the prisoners who inhabited them. They were also built without any regard to the course of streets or avenues. There were no Broadways or Wall streets, though "stocks" were always in the market, not petroleum or bank, but Exchange and Escape, which, at that time, were of vastly more importance to us. Stocks in Exchange were frequently several hundred per cent above par, but in one hour would go tumbling down far below, when none but the *very* "fresh fish" would invest.

Escape stocks were not susceptible of such wonderful contraction and expansion, and run more regular, being always above par, and during the first two months at Camp Sorghum (the name given this prison in honor of the large quantity of molasses of that description issued us at this place) over three hundred Yankee officers realized on it. Many more tried their fortunes, but had been recaptured; in fact, they were escaping and being brought back every day.

Tunneling, bribing the guards, and all the old dodges heretofore alluded to, were tried; and of extremely dark nights, it was a wise precaution of the prisoners to keep close to mother earth, as at such times balls from the guns of the sentinels on duty were constantly whizzing over the camp, having been hurriedly discharged by the excited sentinels, over whose beats adventurous and daring Yankees were constantly passing.

Two of our officers, attempting to gain their freedom in this way, were killed and several wounded; and one night they killed two of their own men. Sometimes from three hundred to four hundred prisoners were paroled to go outside the guard-line after wood, which gave a favorable opportunity for large numbers to escape in the following manner: Those who had not taken the parole, would mix in with those who had done so, and after getting in the woods, their friends would cover them with boughs or leaves, and there secreted, they would remain until after dark, when they would emerge from their hiding places and strike off through the swamps for "God's country." As many as one hundred officers have escaped in one day in this way, but the distance to our lines was so great, and the citizens through the country were ever on the alert with blood-hounds to hunt them down, so that at least seventy-five per cent. of all that escaped from prison, were recaptured and brought back.

CHAPTER XI

ESCAPE OF CAPTAIN RUSSELL

The following interesting and graphic sketch, is Captain M. T. Russell's account of his escape and perilous adventures through the mountainous districts of Georgia. and South Carolina, en route to the Union lines. He was one of the number who escaped from Camp Sorghum, as recorded in the last chapter.

Failing to make my escape when Colonel Streight made his exit from Libby, very much discouraged me, and for some time I gave up all hopes of ever getting away from my prison home, unless the Government should change its policy in regard to the exchange of prisoners, an event which I had no idea would take place us long as Mr. Stanton was retained as Secretary of War. Twelve months had now elapsed since I entered the Libby prison. The work of conquering the rebellion was rapidly progressing in the West; Vicksburg had fallen, and the Mississippi river was open for the navigation of our transports from its source to the Gulf of Mexico; our armies were also making rapid inroads into Georgia, the empire State of the "Confederacy," and General Grant, after having accomplished this great work, was appointed to the command .of the Army of the Potomac, an event which satisfied the prisoners - especially those belonging to the western army, who knew the kind of metal Ulysses was composed of - that the rebel authorities would not long risk keeping us confined in Richmond, Consequently hope began to revive in the bosoms of those who expected to gain their freedom by their own exertion.

Plans for escape, in case of removal, were now being constantly projected and discussed, but no unity or organization for a general outbreak could he arrived at, consequently each one was left to act independently and on his own judgment, and if he thought escape possible, to make the attempt.

At one o'clock on the morning of :May seventh, we were ordered to get ready to march, and one hour given us to accomplish the work, at the end of which they commenced counting us out at the narrow door, and, as though we were so many hogs, the rebel Commissary pitched a pone of corn bread at each of us as we passed. As we came out we were placed between two long files ·of guards, running along Carey street, where we remained until the sun came up from behind the Richmond hills - the first time we felt his warm rays for twelve weary months. we were then marched to the Danville depot, and packed into old stock cars for transportation, sixty odd prisoners and five guards in each car. The weather was extremely hot, water very scarce and "grub" ditto; and in this condition we travelled to Danville, Virginia, twenty-four hours' journey, during which time we received water but twice, and but one half pint each time, and that taken from a pond so filthy that a hog would scarcely wallow in it. After being removed from the train at Danville, the rebel officers were very much chagrined to find that the Yanks had cut large holes in the bottom of the cars, and several of the "d-nd rascals" (as they were pleased to call them,) gone.

From Richmond to Danville the guard in charge of us was commanded by a scoundrel in the shape of a man, whom they called Captain. From his deportment and treatment of the prisoners on the route, all concurred in the opinion that if the devil had any agents, that this man Tabb was certainly one of his chiefs, if not, his majesty bad better "close business on this terrestrial sphere.

We were kept at Danville but a few days, when we were again jammed in cars, (sixty or seventy in each,) and started further South, and arrived at Macon, Georgia, on the sixteenth day of May, 1864, and placed in a stockade for safe keeping. We at once organized squads and companies and commenced tunneling passages underground, through which to escape, and had several large ones nearly completed, when one of our own officers betrayed our work and plans to the Confederate authorities, who soon placed a check on our operations.

In July we were removed to Charleston, An admirable plan for escape on the route was organized by those of us who went on the first train, but those who were appointed to lead and direct the affair, had not the courage to lead off. We were kept at Charleston nearly three months of the hottest season of the year, and all the time under the fire of our own guns. This unprecedented measure of the rebels was done for the purpose of compelling the Government to an exchange of prisoners on terms proposed by themselves, but experience taught them that the United States was not to be dictated to by rebels.

During the fall the yellow fever made its appearance among the prisoners, in consequence of which we were removed to the city of Columbia, where we were placed in an old field, with a single guard line around us. Now I thought, was my time to make another effort to reach "God's country," (the Union lines, being so termed by the prisoners,) and at once began operating on the guards, and soon found that if I was cautious, and selected a good subject, that I could bribe him with a watch, or a few Confederate dollars, to let me pass out. The greatest difficulty that presented itself was, how could I subsist in a strange land, where I dare not stop at the house of a white man, as immediate arrest and confinement would be my inevitable doom. It would not do for the eye of a white man, woman or child, to see me, as legions of blood-hounds, double barreled shot-guns, old men and .boys, conscript officers and Provost Marshals, would at once be in pursuit; besides, it was at least four hundred miles to the Union lines, by the shortest route that could be taken, and my clothing was much worn, and very thin; I was without good shoes, and at this season of the year I could but expect cold weather, even in South Carolina, and much severer when I reached the mountains. Rivers and large streams were also to be crossed, and I knew that all the principal bridges and fords were guarded by the enemy, for the purpose of catching deserters from their own army, and runaway negroes. Notwithstanding all these difficulties, I determined on making another effort to gain my freedom, even if it should cost me my life - " Liberty or Death," was now my motto. In the first place, I must raise the wherewithal to bribe the sentinel, and on making a thorough examination of my *valuables*, I found them to consist of one pocket comb, a brass button, silver penholder and gold pen point; these constituted my store of worldly goods, :and with them I proceeded to drive a bargain with one of the chivalry and escape their clutches for a short time, at least. We had an opportunity of conversing with the guards when they came in to attend roll call, and on one of these occasions I selected a boy from one of the companies, and proceeded to form an acquaintance with him. At first he was not very communicative, but I directed the conversation in regard to his manner of procuring subsistence, asking him if he lived exclusively on the rations furnished by the rebel Commissary. He replied that he was compelled to do it, as he was without money wherewith to procure anything else. I remarked to him that I had a good gold pen and silver holder, both worth at least one hundred and fifty dollars in. Confederate money, and which I would give him if he would let me pass his beat some dark night. He finally agreed to the proposition, provided I would promise on honor not to betray him in case I was re-captured and brought back, to which I of course agreed, and began preparations for my departure. From a friend who had sold his watch to one of the guards, I borrowed ten dollars in Confederate money. With this I purchased from the Sutler one quart of salt, and some matches; I also baked my five days' rations of corn-meal, which, when done, made about three pounds of bread. For a haversack to carry it in, I took an old flannel shirt and tied the lower extremity with a string, like a bag, and the sleeves together, to swing over my shoulder.

    Three days after, the soldier with whom the arrangement was made, guarded me with several others outside the lines, to procure wood for fuel. The same morning, however, a large number of the prisoners were put on parole of honor not to escape, by the Commandant of the prison, and allowed to go out for the same purpose. Soon as a favorable opportunity offered for me to pass the guard whom I had bribed, without being observed by the other sentinels, I stepped up to him and gave him the pen and pen-holder, and passed out and made a straight line for the nearest pine thicket, almost fearing to look back lest I was observed by others of the rebel guard, and by them returned to the prison.

    I traveled through the thicket about four miles, when I came to a swamp, I went into this several hundred yards, and found a large pine log laying up out of the water, upon which I crawled, intending to remain there until after dark, but I had not long been concealed here until I heard some one walking through the water. From the direction whence the noise proceeded, and its gradual nearer approach, I supposed that it was the rebels on my track, and quietly as possible slipped off the log on the opposite side from the direction the sound came, I had been in this position but a short time when I discovered approaching me, instead of an armed rebel with a pack of blood-hounds, one of my old prison companions, Lieutenant Frank A. Lakin, of the Eighteenth Indiana Infantry, an officer with whom I had been confined in the various prisons of the Confederacy for one year and a half. I knew that he would do to depend upon in the perilous and toilsome work before us; young, active, brave and full of fire, and when be once made up his mind to do a thing he never gave it up until it had been accomplished, unless some unavoidable streak of bad fortune interposed. There was no officer among all the prisoners with whom I had, been confined that I would have preferred as a companion on the hazardous journey before me. We consulted together as to the best route to be taken to reach our lines, Soon as it was dark we started out, intending to strike the road leading from Columbia to Lexington; we had not traveled far, however, when the sky became very much clouded, obscuring the north star, by which we were directing our course, but we continued to travel, without guide or compass, until about two o'clock in the morning, when the clouds cleared away, and we discovered that we were going in the wrong direction, We accordingly changed our course, and again set out for the road before mentioned, and which we finally found. We traveled very cautiously for some considerable distance, and at length came to a guide-board, which we hailed with joy, as it was a silent director that would not betray us; it was so dark, however, that it availed us nothing without some little ingenuity, so I squared myself in front of the post with my hands on my knees and with my shoulders stooped over, while Frank mounted my back, crawled up and struck a match and examined the directions on the board, when he discovered that we were just five miles from Columbia and seven miles from Lexington, and had traveled hard all night; but we determined, if possible, to pass the latter place before daylight - the grey streaks of light just making their appearance in the east when we came to the suburbs of the village. We now held a council of war, and decided that our best plan was to go direct through town, so we walked very briskly up Maine street, encountering on the way several noisy dogs, which alarmed us considerably, lest they should be the means of arousing the citizens, as lights were already visible in many of the houses; but we passed through safely, and soon came to a dense pine thicket, into which we went some two or three hundred yards and stopped near a large pond, where we raked some leaves together for a bed and lay down tired and foot-sore to rest, and did not awake until near sunset.

After making a hasty toilet by washing in the pond and drying our faces on the leaves and dead grass: we sat down to partake of my loaf of corn bread which still remained untouched, and as neither of us had tasted a morsel for twenty-four hours, it was very palatable. At dark we again started on the road, and when we came near a house always flanked it, so as not to be observed by the dogs. We traveled all night, and next morning went into the woods again, to conceal ourselves, and rest and sleep; but we were so hungry that sleep with me was impossible. While pondering where our next provisions were to come from, I suddenly heard the noise of a bell and bleating of sheep. I remarked to my friend Frank that we had better capture and slaughter one, as we could live very well on its flesh, even if we had no bread. He thought it would be impossible to catch one of them, and turned over in the leaves to sleep, But Frank's opinion to the contrary notwithstanding, I, was determined to have some mutton for breakfast, and gathered my salt bag and started toward the sheep. Salt being a luxury to which rebel sheep had not been of late accustomed, the whole flock was soon collected around me, some licking salt from my hands. Just at this moment Frank raised up, and seeing that the prospect for mutton was very good, yelled out: "Catch a *fat* one, Milt." I made a *grab* and caught a very nice lamb. Soon as he discovered that I had secured the prize, he started toward me at the rate of "2:40" with the old case knife, with which we soon dispatched the juvenile sheep, and when dressed found it to be very fat and tender. we had no water to either wash our hands or mutton, but we kindled a fire and a portion of the carcass was soon on it roasting, and the savory slices of mutton alone, made us a delightful breakfast; after which we lay down to sleep, and did not awake until near sunset.

We immediately commenced preparations for another night's march, but before starting we cut out the best pieces remaining of the lamb's carcass, and put them in my haversack for our subsistence the next day, We had not traveled far before we both felt the evil effects of eating so much meat without bread, and Frank swore " by the Eternal" he would never taste mutton again. Journeyed all night without any incident of note. About daylight in the morning we came to a secluded place, where we went into bivouac, and lay down to sleep without eating, the breakfast of the previous morning still weighing heavy on our stomachs. When we awoke up in the evening, and before starting on the tramp, Frank remarked that he believed "he could eat a little more of that sheep," provided it was cooked in any other manner than by being broiled on the coals.

Before it was quite dark we were again on the tramp, and early in the evening, while flanking a large farm house that stood near the road, we accidentally found ourselves - very much to our satisfaction - in a sweet potato patch, and at once set about digging the precious roots, about a half bushel of which we tied up in Frank's old jacket, and proceeded to the next plantation. Near one of the huts we discovered a negro woman washing by the burning light of a few pine faggots collected in a pile by her side. We remained in concealment watching her for about twenty minutes, when she started off towards the house. We then cautiously approached the fire, and Frank shouldered the kettle she had been using and carried it off about a mile to a pond, surrounded by a dense thicket, and it was not long ere we had it swung over a bright fire of blazing pine knots, filled with a goodly quantity of sweet potatoes and the remains of our mutton. In about two hours later we were partaking of one of the most delicious feasts of food to which I ever sat down. Frank's forty-eight hours' fasting had entirely obliterated from his mind the memory of his vow not to eat sheep. After partaking to our satisfaction, we filled our haversacks with the remainder and started on the march, forgetting, however, to return the old woman's kettle.

As near as possible, we kept a direct course for Knoxville. Before we left the prison at Columbia I procured an old pocket-map of the Southern States, of which I made a copy on a sheet of foolscap paper. It was, of course, very incorrect, but answered our purpose, as it gave us some idea of the distances from point to point, and the localities of the principal towns. We still followed the old plan of traveling after night, and laying by in the woods and thickets during the day time.

Three days and nights thus passed without incident or adventure of any kind, at the end of which we found our commissary department in a very unfavorable Condition for promoting the health and strength of two ravenous individuals as Frank and myself. It was the third morning after we had boiled the mutton and potatoes before mentioned, that we were aroused from our slumbers by the side of a fire we had built, by the neighing of a horse. We both instantly sprang to our feet, and about one hundred .yards distant discovered a negro coming towards us on horse-back, drawn hither, as we afterwards learned, by the smoke of our fire. He came up to within a few yards of us and then suddenly stopped, evidently considerably frightened; and, although we had determined not to reveal ourselves to anyone, either black or white, we at once saw that we must make friends with this man, and accordingly entered into conversation with him and informed him of our true character. He solemnly promised not to betray us to his master, but on the contrary pledged himself to assist us in every way in his power. We told him that we were very hungry, and out of provisions. He then left us, but returned in about an hour, bringing with him a basket full of roasted potatoes and a small piece of corn bread, saying, that was all he had, but we were welcome to have it. He was very intelligent, and during our conversation with him, remarked that as we were sacrificing so much for the freedom of him and his race, he thought it no more than his duty to do all in his power for our safety and comfort. He also gave us much information in regard to the roads and country, and with tearful eyes bid us good.bye. The provisions he gave us lasted two days, after which we were one day without anything to eat, and were consequently getting so hungry that I proposed making a foray on some plantation and steal something, but Frank stoutly protested against thieving since the stolen sheep he had partaken so heartily of had made him sick.

    We traveled two nights without anything to eat except a few persimmons, and was now on the road the third day almost exhausted from hunger and fatigue, but, about ten o'clock, we came to a large plantation; we then halted and held a council of war, when it was decided to cautiously approach one of the negro huts, from which the whizzing sound of a large spinning wheel in motion, proceeded; we stealthily crawled up, and, through a chink in the wall, could discover a negro woman spinning cotton; we then went around to the opposite side of the house, and knocked at the door, Upon which interruption the wheel suddenly stopped, and the old woman cried out, "Who's dat?" We replied, in a low tone, that we were friends, and requested her to let us in, when she yelled out, "Who's dat at de door? " We replied, as before, and finally persuaded her to open the door, when we stepped in, and Frank proceeded to tell her that we were Confederate soldiers on furlough, nearly starved, and wanted something to eat; while he was speaking the old negress interrupted him, saying, "Gemen, you can't fool dis chile; I knows who you is'; I knows you is Yankees, 'cause I see de buttons on dat jacket," pointing to Frank's old blue blouse which served the double purpose of coat and shirt, and which still retained two or three brass buttons, the same as worn on the uniform of the United States soldiers. 'We acknowledged to her that we were escaped Union prisoners; she then set to work, and, in a short time, prepared a bountiful supply of corn-bread and roasted sweet potatoes; she also set before us a fine, fat opossum, nicely baked, and, between Frank and myself, we made that 'possum disappear in a very short time.

All the darkies on the plantation came in to see us, bringing with them, for us, their little mite of provisions. After we had finished our suppers and rested our weary limbs, one of the darkies volunteered his services to pilot us ten miles on the road, which we gladly accepted. After the ten miles had been gone over, he turned us over to another negro who went with us about five miles; by this time it was nearly daylight, and we were placed by the last guide under the care of a third negro who conducted us about one half mile to a dense pine thicket, where we lay concealed during the day.

Soon after dark our negro protector returned, and with him nearly a dozen men and women of his own color, each bringing something for us to eat; they had corn-meal, coffee, corn-cake, fresh pork, sweet potatoes and cabbage; to us it was truly a feast, and we done it ample justice.

Before starting on the road, we took each of these ignorant, but loyal and zealous colored people, by the hand, and bid them a kind and friendly good by; in fact, the saves were the only class of people we could call friends, in the whole State of South Carolina.

The third day after parting with the crowd of negroes last referred to, we were discovered by a white man, the first white face we had seen since leaving the prison. The old man came on us accidentally, and was about as much alarmed at the collision as we were, but my friend, Lieutenant Lakin, volunteered to act as spokesman, and confidently rushed out towards the intruder on our privacy with extended hand. The old man, after gaining his self-possession questioned Frank pretty closely, but he replied promptly and apparently satisfactorily, and stated to him that we belonged to General Lee's army, and had been in service since the beginning of the war; that when our enlistment expired, we were promised thirty days furlough if we would re-enlist, and that we did so, but the leave of absence was never granted, and we had, consequently, resolved to go, without permission, and see our families who were at home suffering; that we intended to remain there just thirty days, and would not be taken back in less time by any d--d home guards in South Carolina,

We then appealed to the old man's sympathies, when he said that he did not blame us, and promised that he would do nothing to betray us; and I believe the old fellow kept his promise, for we remained there all day without further molestation,

The next night, about twelve o'clock, we met two negroes in the road, who informed us that two miles further ahead there was a company of Confederate soldiers watching for deserters: we accordingly left the road, and, taking the North star for our guide, we proceeded through swamps and over hills until we came to Broad river; this we must cross at all hazards, and the only alternative was to wade and swim; so, into the cold, rapid stream we plunged, the water striking us around the neck, and so chilly that I thought we would freeze before reaching the opposite bank, but we got through safely, and started oft' on a brisk walk, which soon got up a circulation, and we felt quite comfortable "barrin" a little *dampness*.

We now felt quite safe, and began to talk earnestly of the happy hours we would soon enjoy with the "loved ones at home." "But man proposes and God disposes." The following night, while resting in a thicket, two or three hundred yards from the road on which we had been traveling, we were suddenly startled by the loud yelping of hounds not a great distance from us. We knew, at once, that they were on our track, but as we had left the road by a right angle, we had hope that the dogs would here lose the scent, and keep the main road, but we reckoned without our host, for, in a moment, the whole pack, of at least a dozen fierce looking bloodhounds were upon us; escape was now impossible, for any attempt to move would have caused the dogs to take immediate hold of our persons.

While in this dilemma, about twenty-five of the chivalry made their appearance, armed with shot-guns, knives, pistols and clubs; they at once made a peremptory demand for us to surrender, and not feeling able to combat successfully both dogs and men, we at once complied with the modest request.

The manner and bearing of these Southern cavaliers towards us after we were in their power was disgusting in the extreme. They seemed to think that they bad accomplished one of the most gallant deeds of the war, and declared they would never submit to "Yankee rule,"

Ropes were brought out to tie our hands and feet, but, after searching us thoroughly, and satisfying themselves that we had no arms, they concluded that there were enough of the party to guard us to Anderson jail without adopting this measure. They marched us to Anderson court-house, seventeen miles distant, when they turned us over to the provost marshal of the district, who confined us in the jail at that place for five days; and while there we had many calls from the citizens, both men and women, whose curiosity to see a " real live Yankee" prompted them to make the visits; the negroes, also, were anxious to see us, and one evening some half dozen of them were permitted by the jailor to come in where we were; they had a violin in the party, upon which they gave us several very cheering airs. Lieutenant Lakin being somewhat of a musician, took the instrument in his hands, and, to the great delight of the darkies, gave them a touch of "Yankee Doodle." When ready to depart, they insisted on the jailor for permission to leave the fiddle with us. We could not understand the reason of this strange request, and our curiosity was, consequently, somewhat aroused; so, after being left to ourselves, we made a thorough examination of the instrument, when, to our great surprise and delight, we found inside of it, thirty-nine dollars (Confederate currency) secreted there by the negroes for our benefit.

On the morning of the seventh day of our incarceration in the jail at this place, we were taken out, and, under heavy guard, sent back to our old quarters at Camp Sorghum, Columbia. Notwithstanding the blustering threats of the rebel officials to severely punish any prisoner who made a second attempt at escape, we resolved on another effort to reach the Union lines whenever opportunity offered. Before we got ready for the second trial, the following order was communicated to the prisoners then confined in Camp Sorghum:

"Headquarters, S. C., Georgia and Florida, Charleston, November 17th, 1864.

Colonel Means, Commanding Federal Prisoners at Columbia: The Lieutenant General directs that you report to these headquarters the name of every officer and man who escapes from your custody; also, that you notify the Federal officers that they must give their parole not to attempt to escape, or they will be confined in a pen in the same manner the privates now are.

Very Respectfully,
Your Ob't Serv't,
R. C. GILCHRIS, Acting Ass't Adj't Gen'l."

We at first feared that the majority of our fellow prisoners would be in favor of taking the parole designated in the above order, in which case we would also be obliged to do likewise, or be placed in a position where escape would be impossible, and death, ere long, inevitable. No attention, however, was paid to the order, and the status of the prisoners remained as before. The want of a pen, no doubt, being the only reason that it was not carried into effect.

In a few days I had arrangements all completed for a second escape from rebel custody. With a portion of my share of the money the negroes smuggled to us while in jail at Anderson courthouse, I bought from the sutler a few matches and a pint of salt, after which I had remaining, in good rebel shinplasters, ten dollars, with which I bribed a guard to let me pass his beat, I agreeing to keep the contract strictly secret, and to crawl on my hands and feet from the dead line out beyond the line of guards, and, before starting, to pitch a rock towards him as a signal that I was ready, when, if all was right, he would pitch it back. With this understanding, a short time after dark, the appointed evening, I started from my hut to the designated spot for me to pass out. I walked up to as near the dead line as I dare go, and stopped; it was very dark, and raining, and I could scarcely see ten feet from where I stood; but I pitched a rock as per agreement towards the place I thought the

A Yankee in Rebel Prisons

guard ought to be, I then got down close to the ground and remained perfectly still until a rock, the welcome messenger that announced that all was well, came splashing through the mire towards me. I hesitated not a moment, but started on "all fours" through the mud for the sentinel, who, simultaneously commenced whistling the popular air of "Dixie;" whether it was to drown the pangs of a guilty conscience, or to keep up my spirits, I am not able to say, but freely confess that I felt very much the need of something to bolster up my courage, for I feared he might let me approach within a few feet of him and then fire at me; but I kept on, and finally got up to where the fellow was standing, and handed him the money; he merely remarked, as he received it, that I must not fool him, as some of the other prisoners had done, who, instead of giving him money as they passed out, handed him a roll of old paper.

I continued to crawl on my hands and feet for some distance before assuming an erect position, and when I did so, I started off and run for about two hundred yards at a speed that would throw Flora Temple's best time far in the shade, I then sat down in the bushes and began pondering over "the situation;" no money, scarcely any clothing, no provisions, and no friends. While thus meditating. and feeling very blue, I was startled by the sound of some one walking through the bushes, I instantly dropped on the ground to conceal myself from observation; as the object making the noise drew nearer, I could distinguish that the person, be he who he might, was a Federal officer, bent on the same object as myself. I then arose to my feet, and addressing him in a low tone, inquired who he was? This was such a sudden surprise that he jumped as if he had been shot at, but when he discovered that I was alone, he stopped and confronted me, and behold! who should it be but my old friend and former companion, Frank Lakin! It was a very unexpected meeting to both of us, and we decided to travel together, and over the same route we went before - Knoxville being the point at which we aimed to strike the Union lines. It was a long distance, but, from the information we had, it seemed to us the safest route to freedom. Our plans and direction thus resolved on, we started on the long, weary journey, and traveled the whole night in a cold, chilly rain. We journeyed on for several nights over the same roads that we had marched before. Our experience had been such that we were now fully posted in regard to the best manner for escaped Yankee prisoners traveling in the South to procure provisions, and now had no difficulty in keeping our commissary department well supplied, or, rather the negroes did for us; for, from them we procured everything we wanted to eat; if not always as dainty as might be desired, it was, at least, palatable and wholesome, and, by trusting implicitly on the slaves, we had no difficulty in getting abundance.

When within a few miles of Anderson court-house, the place where we had been confined in jail, after our recapture on the previous expedition we had made in this direction, we met an old negro in the road and informed him who we were and where we were going; he then told us of General Sherman's movements in Georgia, adding that he was "bound to take Augusta," and advised us to change our course, and try to get to Sherman's army. He also told us that he was going to start for Augusta next morning with a wagon and six-mule team, and that he could conceal us in the wagon-bed under the fodder, and haul us safely to the city. We consented to his proposition, and lay concealed in a thicket near the barn until nearly daylight, when we were aroused up by the old negro, who was preparing to leave for that city. We got in his wagon, and were covered up with the fodder, the whip was applied to the mules, and we were off: The road was full of militia, on their route to Augusta also, to which place they were going, as they said, to help defend it against "Sherman's host of blue bellies."

We had not gone but a few miles before we caught up with a regiment of infantry; several stragglers belonging to it got on the wagon - they on top of the fodder, and we underneath - was not very comfortable to us, but we had to "grin and bear it," and in this position we rode until night, making about twenty miles during the day. Shortly after dark the regiment which had been traveling with us all day, went into camp, and the wagon was then cleared of rebel soldiers; the darkey drove on a mile further, and we also went into bivouac near the road.

The next morning we again crawled in the wagon, and was again covered with the fodder, and started out before daylight in advance of the rebel troops, who had been a source of so much annoyance to us the day before. About four o'clock in the afternoon, when within a few miles of Augusta, we were met by a squad of rebel soldiers; our negro friend inquired of them, "If de Yankees got Augusta yet;" they replied in the negative, and wanted to know why he asked the question. The negro replied that he was "Mighty 'feard dem ar Yankees was in de town."

This conversation ended, the soldier's passed on, and, after they had got well out of sight, we jumped out of the wagon and went into the woods, the darkey driving on to Augusta.. We crossed the Savannah river seven miles above the city, and soon after struck the railroad running from Atlanta to Augusta; here we came in contact with another negro from whom we learned that Sherman was at Milledgeville; he also gave us a copy of the Augusta Daily Chronicle, and from what we learned from it, we drew the conclusion that Sherman's intended destination was Savannah, and, consequently, the best plan for us to adopt, would be to flank Augusta, and get some position in advance of Sherman's forces, and then lay by at the hut of some friendly negro until our army came up; with this intention we traveled that night and next day, making a complete circle of the city, and again striking the Savannah river fifteen miles below it; here we procured an old canoe and tried navigation, but it leaked so badly that we were compelled to abandon it and travel by land, and next day we arrived at Millen, the junction of the Macon and Savannah with the Augusta railroad; here we learned from a negro some additional particulars in regard to the march of "Mr. Sherman's company," who, he informed us, had passed there nearly a week previous; we were, consequently, in Sherman's rear instead of his front as we had anticipated, and had to travel seventy-five miles over the same country that his immense army had passed.

The first twenty-four hours on this route convinced us that we would have great difficulty obtaining provisions, as corn-meal, bacon, sweet potatoes and everything else that could be eat, had been pressed by Sherman's hungry Yankees; the negroes had also nearly all followed the army, so that we could no longer obtain subsistence from them, nor their invaluable services as guides. We were suffering extremely from hunger, when we fortunately found two ears of corn in a fence corner, where a cavalry soldier had fed his horse. We built a fire and parched it on the cob, and with the addition of a little salt, made a very excellent meal.

The fourth night we traveled in this direction we came to a wide slough, over which had been a railroad bridge, but whose black and charred timbers now floated on top of the stagnant stream; a number of these we collected together and proceeded to construct a raft on which to cross to the opposite bank; when completed, a piece of telegraph wire was fastened to It, and my traveling companion, Frank, got aboard, pushed it out in the stream, and soon landed safely on the other side of the water. With the piece of wire attached to it, one end of which I held in, my hand, I pulled the frail craft back to my side, got on board, and started over to rejoin Frank, but, when near the middle of the stream, the treacherous craft split in two parts, and much to the gusto of Lakin, let me to the neck in the cold, icy water; but I was more alarmed for Frank than myself, as his violent laughter at my sudden immersion gave me sufficient grounds to fear a collapse in the vicinity of his commissary department.

I finally waded out safe and whole, though terribly wet and cold. Our situation was now very critical, and required the exercise of the greatest caution on our part; otherwise we were almost certain to be recaptured, as Wheeler's cavalry was now between us and our own army. The night following my adventures by water, when, as just related, I was suddenly shipwrecked, we were met in the road by a slave, who had just escaped from Wheeler's command. Our fortunate meeting with this faithful fellow, no doubt, saved us our liberty, for we were then within a half mile of the rebel pickets, and had we not met with him, would have soon been close on them, when it would be too late to escape.

Regardless of his own personal safety, this black man, true to the instinct of his race, cheerfully consented to pilot us around Wheeler's pickets, which was successfully accomplished by wading and crawling for two hours through the miasmatic swamps of the Georgia lowland, and after passing safely around the rebel lines we selected an elevated spot of ground in the interior of a large swamp, where we lay down to rest and sleep until night.

Frank was soon in the land of dreams, but for my part I could not sleep. I had an ill foreboding that all was not right, so instead of sleeping I kept watch, and near noon I discovered a man preceded by two large blood-hounds, coming towards us. Their company, of course, was not at all desirable, but it seemed that there was no way of avoiding it, as they still advanced nearer, and there was no way for us to get out of the swamp except by the route they were coming. I awoke Lakin and asked his opinion of the situation. We concluded that it was best to remain perfectly quiet, and in case we were attacked to defend ourselves to the last, as we had resolved that no one man should take us alive. The following programme was agreed upon: we both had heavy walking sticks, and Frank was to engage the intruder in conversation, at the same time I would step up behind him and give him such a blow with my stick that he would never disturb another Yankee. By the time this plan was decided upon, the stranger was within forty yards of where we lay concealed, and keeping straight forward in the direction he was going would pass a few yards to the left of us. We were beginning to think ourselves quite safe, and that the man would pass on without noticing us, when one of the hounds, snuffing the air, set up a terrible *bo-hoo* and he turned to look after the dogs, and discovered us. We instantly jumped up and endeavored to engage him in conversation, but the nearer we approached him the faster he walked, till at length he struck a brisk trot, and soon disappeared in the dense pine thicket. We dared not remain longer here, as we knew this fellow would soon alarm the whole neighborhood, when all the old men and boys, furloughed soldiers, negroes and dogs in the country, would be in pursuit. Consequently, we changed our base, establishing ourselves, as we thought, in a more secure place in another swamp; but we had not occupied this new line of defense long when we heard in the distance the well-known *toot* of the hunter's horn, which apprised us of the fact that they were preparing for the chase, and ere long we distinctly heard the whining bark of the hounds and yells of the men, as they came in hot pursuit, till they arrived at the edge of the water where we entered, which broke the scent, and they could track us no further. From our concealed position we could see every movement they made; in the posse we counted fifteen men, but the number of hounds was beyond computation.

The party at length divided and started in opposite directions around the swamp, to discover, if possible, where we left it, not supposing that we were still hid in its dark recesses. Soon as they disappeared we left our place of concealment, and made for the railroad, which we fortunately struck at a point where the track had not been torn up, and here found a hand-car which we took possession of, and started at full speed in the direction of Savannah. We went six miles this way when we had to abandon the car, on account of the track being destroyed. Leaving the car we sought a safe retreat, as usual, in a swamp, where we remained until dark, and again started on the march. This, we confidently hoped, would be our last night's travel, as we were satisfied that we were now so close to Sherman's army that we could reach it, no ill fortune intervening, by daylight next morning. Our strength was nearly exhausted for want of food, but the thought of home and freedom nerved us to the work, and we kept on until about three o'clock in the morning, when we had grown so weak that it seemed impossible to move another rod. We had eaten nothing for four days but the two ears of corn, before mentioned, and now we reeled and staggered like drunken men; we could stand erect no longer, and fell exhausted by the side of the road, so fatigued that sleep soon overcome us.

About daylight we were aroused by the sound of reveille on the drums in Sherman's camps; this was music so sweet, and sent such a thrill of joy through our hearts, that we forgot hungry stomachs, weary limbs and sore feet, and we sprang lightly up and started with light hearts, to the camp of the Union army. Two hours' march brought us to the picket line of General Sherman's army – language fails to express my feelings, when, for the first time in nearly two years, I beheld the glorious old flag.

We were conducted to General Sherman's headquarters, and were kindly received by him and the officers of his staff. The General provided us with clothing and provisions, and also furnished us transportation to the City of Washington. *We were free now, and no thanks to E. M. Stanton, for our liberty.*

MILTON T. RUSSELL,
Captain Fifty-First Indiana Volunteers.

CHAPTER XII

REMOVAL FROM CAMP SORGHUM.

Although we were set down in this place the first of October without shelter or habitation of any kind, and without tools or material to construct any sort of protection against the chilling wintry blast, yet by the first of December, by indefatigable energy and perseverance, assisted by our Yankee ingenuity, we had built a city that could boast as many styles of architecture as Gotham itself. Axes, spades and hatchets, were bought at enormous prices from the rebel guards, and of our scant allowance of wood for fuel, we saved out the best *building timber* of which frames were made, and covered with dirt and leaves. Our huts and cabins constructed, we were settling down into comparatively comfortable winter quarters; too much so, the rebel officials thought, for the welfare of Yankee prisoners, and through the malignant nature of our keepers we were removed to the vacant grounds connected with the Insane Asylum, in the city of Columbia. Here we were again without shelter, and thinly clad exposed to stormy winds, rain and frost; and this, too, after those of us who were able to do a stroke of work had assiduously employed the months of October and November erecting winter quarters. It is true a few thousand feet of lumber was here given us, also tools to build barracks, but when we left there in February, there had not been lumber enough furnished to shelter one hundred and fifty men, leaving nearly one thousand without quarters, except such as they procured and erected without assistance from the authorities having us in charge.

We suffered extremely while in the "Asylum Prison" for want of fuel, one small stick per day for each mess of five being all that was allowed us. Our rations while in Columbia were also inferior in quality and less in quantity than we had before received at any of the prisons in which we had been confined; two-thirds of a pint of coarse corn-meal, grain and cob both ground together and unbolted, and a gill of sorghum molasses for each man, was all that we received for a day's ration. Not an ounce of meat during the whole winter did they issue us - it was corn for breakfast, corn for dinner, and corn for supper, if we had any, which was seldom, for two scant meals per day was as much as our rations would furnish.

Some of the officers, while here, had small amounts of money forwarded to them by their friends in the North. Gold and greenbacks were retained in the hands of the rebel authorities, and they would occasionally give to the parties to whom such monies were credited a few dollars in Confederate money, saying that so much of their gold had been converted by the Quartermaster into that kind of currency for his (the prisoner's) use. But even in this currency we were never allowed more than one-half the price that gold was worth, or rather selling for, in Jeff Davis's promises to pay, on the streets. For instance, if a gold dollar was worth one hundred Confederate dollars at the broker's office, the prisoners would get from the authorities about fifty dollars. But a still greater imposition, practiced on us, both at Columbia and Charleston, was the following: parties were sent into the prison with bundles of the trash called Confederate money, which they distributed at the rate of two dollars for one of greenbacks, and six dollars for one of gold, which was paid in drafts on our friends in the North. Notwithstanding these exorbitant rates the famishing prisoners were glad of the opportunity of thus getting the money, with which, worthless as it was, we could purchase from the Sutler a little salt and meat, and occasionally a few vegetables; these, however, were as dear as the money we paid for them. The day before I left Columbia I bought ten pounds of bacon, for which I paid one hundred and ten dollars; a pair of coarse, half made shoes, one hundred and thirty-five dollars; a pint of salt, two dollars, and a box of matches, one dollar and fifty cents.

Our amusements in the "Asylum Prison" varied but little from what they had been in the other places in which we bad been confined, except to the various games we had previously played with cards, was now added, since the introduction of the money above referred to, the game of faro, Great attention was also devoted to music, and "Chandler's String Band" was an institution connected with our prison life that will never be forgotten, Its soul-stirring strains were indelibly impressed on the memory of the heart-sore and desponding prisoners, whose gloomy hours were cheered by the sweet notes of "Home, Sweet Home," "Hail Columbia," "The Star Spangled Banner," and many other sentimental and national airs. The instruments used by the above named band were purchased by the prisoners in Charleston, and consisted of a bass viol, two violins and a flute, costing an average of three hundred dollars each, which, exorbitant as it is, was in consideration of the potent influence they exercised as sanitary agents, a good investment, I have seen many a poor sufferer, whom no persuasion of friends could induce to leave his pallet, arise and hobble out to where the band was discoursing "We are Coming, Father Abraham," "Yankee Doodle," or "Down with the Traitor," Adjutant :Byer's "Sherman's March to the Sea" was also one of the most popular airs among the prisoners, Being composed in prison by one of our own number, all seemed to take an unusual interest in it; and, on this account, as well as for its beautiful sentiment, I insert the poem in this volume:

SHERMAN'S MARCH TO THE SEA
By Lieutenant Byers, Fifth Iowa Cavalry

Our camp tires shone bright on the mountain,

A Yankee in Rebel Prisons

That frowned on the river below,
While we stood by our guns in the morning
And eagerly watched for the foe,
When a rider came out of the darkness

That hung over mountain and tree,
And shouted "Boys, up and be ready,"
For Sherman will march to the sea."

Then shout after shout for bold Sherman
Went up from each valley and glen,
And the bugles re-echoed the music
That fell from the lips of the men;
For we knew that the stars on our banner
More bright in their splendor would be,
And that blessings from Northland would greet us
When Sherman marched down to the sea.

Then forward boys, forward to battle;
We marched on our wearisome way,
And we stormed the wild hill of Resaca
God bless those who fell on that day
Then Kenesaw, dark in his glory,
Looked down on the flag of the free,
But the East and the West bore our standard
When Sherman marched down to the sea.

Still onward we pressed, till our banners
Swept out from Atlanta's grim walls,
And the blood of the patriot dampened
. The soil where the traitor's flag falls.
But we paused not to weep for the fallen
Who slept by each river and tree,
Yet we twined them a wreath of the laurel

A Yankee in Rebel Prisons

As Sherman marched down to the sea..

0, proud was our army that morning
That stood where the pine proudly towers,
When Sherman said - "Boys, you are weary -
This day fair Savannah is ours."

Then sang we a song for our Chieftain
That echoed o'er river and lea,
For the stars in our banner shone brighter
When Sherman had marched to the sea.

ANOTHER MOVE

Slowly passed the weary winter days of 1864 and 1865; the usual dull monotonous routine of everyday life dragged slowly along, and when ended our only consolation was, that we were one day nearer freedom. After the fall of Atlanta and occupation of that city by General Sherman's army, the local newspapers which we had hitherto been allowed to receive, were denied us; sometimes, however, by paying the guard five dollars, he would smuggle one of the Columbia dailies – a brown, dingy half sheet - in camp to us, whose contents, although they could never be regarded as reliable, were eagerly devoured by the anxious prisoners, who were *starving* for *news*, and mental food, as well as physical sustenance. From these papers we learned that Sherman had made a triumphant march through Georgia; had consequently compelled the evacuation of Savannah, and had already with his gallant army, flushed with victory, crossed the Savannah river, and was, early in February, rapidly penetrating the interior of South Carolina. This was to us information as pleasing as any we could desire, except perhaps, the announcement that a "general exchange was agreed upon," for although we were not aware that it was Sherman's intention to sweep through the entire State, we knew from our previous experience that we would not long be allowed to remain in such close proximity to the Union armies; and preparations were accordingly made by most of us to escape from rebel custody whenever the move should come.

On the twelfth of February we had intimations from the authorities that we would be but a few days longer in Columbia; and on the fourteenth, about six hundred of us were taken out of the prison and marched to the Charlotte depot, *packed* in stock car's; and consigned to Charlotte, North Carolina; but a large number, including myself, were "lost in transportation."

The forepart of the day had been remarkably fine and pleasant, even for the mild and genial latitude of South Carolina, but about the middle of the afternoon, and soon after the train left Columbia, a cold, drizzling rain, such as are frequently experienced in the high latitude of New York and Pennsylvania, commenced falling. This was considered especially favorable to the designs of us who contemplated an escape - a dark, misty night being what we most desired to aid us in such an important undertaking.

CHAPTER XIII

OUT OF THE JAWS OF DEATH

Captain John Aigan, Fifth Rhode Island Artillery; Lieutenant James F. Pool, First Virginia Cavalry; Lieutenant H. W. Mosley, and myself, soon as it was known that we were to be removed from Columbia, resolved to escape on the route, together, and accordingly made the usual preparations, which consisted in procuring a supply of matches, salt and pepper, the last named article to be applied to our heels when on the march, for the purpose of breaking the scent of the hounds, which we anticipated would very probably be put on our trail; we had also saved from our small allowance of daily rations a portion for our subsistence on the route, which, before leaving the prison, we carefully packed in Lieutenant Pool's haversack. Everything worked charmingly, and in our favor; without trouble we all got in the same car and secured seats near the door, I should more properly say a standing place, for it must be remembered that Yankee prisoners traveling over Southern railroads, were never put in cars that had comfortable and necessary furniture; but, as I was about to say, we had gained the desired position, and were determined to hold it until a favorable opportunity for leaving the car presented itself. Our friends in the rear whose corns we were treading, and the rebel guards in front whose blankets supplied the place of rugs for our muddy feet, to the contrary notwithstanding.

Thus situated, we traveled for several hours after leaving Columbia, but the reader will bear in mind that we were not aboard a New York or Philadelphia express train, but going at the terrific rate of eight miles an hour over a Southern road, in such a deplorable state of repair that in the North it would not be considered safe to be used even as a side switch to run a construction train over; consequently, when night came, we were only a few miles from the point of our departure, and about eight o'clock P. M. we were standing at a dead halt five miles from Winnsboro, a town of considerable importance on the road between Columbia and Charlotte, the cause of this detention being a break of some part of the engine, and which the engineers were industriously endeavoring to repair. It was now extremely cold and freezing, the drizzling rain which continued to come down all the afternoon and evening had now turned to sleet, and was falling very fast. The guards on top of the cars were so chilled and benumbed as to be almost incapable of using their limbs, while those guarding the door were muffled up in their coats and blankets, and almost entirely unconscious of surrounding objects; but we, although thinner clad, and as much exposed, heeded neither cold, sleet, nor rain. The longing desire for liberty burned within us and kept us warm; we felt that on this night's actions depended our liberties; the golden opportunity was now before us, and we must embrace it.

It was very dark, the train motionless, and the guards in the door half asleep, while those on the top of the car were benumbed with cold. "Now was our time," remarked Lieutenant Mosley, as he quietly and unnoticed worked his way between the two guards in the door, and swung himself down to the ground, I immediately followed him. Alighting on terra firma, we reconnoitered the situation, when we discovered the track where the train was standing was laid on a high embankment, the banks of which sloped down from the rails on either side forty or fifty feet., and were covered with briars, brambles and various kinds of small undergrowth, and through this we were compelled to crawl to get away from the train. When I first descended to the ground, I heard the footsteps of some one approaching; to run, or even move, I felt would lead to a discovery of our escape from the cars, and I therefore stretched myself out full length on the muddy ground. I had scarcely assumed this undignified position, however, when a rebel guard, who bad left one of the rear cars and was going up to the front to see his officer, stumbled and fell squarely over me, his gun falling out of his hands and resting on my arm - thus, at the very moment I wished to be farthest away from rebels and rebel bayonets, I had both in my embrace – but the guard was evidently so stupefied that I had no reason to be much alarmed at this adventure. He soon picked himself and gun up and went on, muttering that he "believed he had fell over somebody;" to me a self evident fact, that needed no assertion of his to prove. Not wishing to be in his way as he returned, I started on "all fours" into the briars and brambles, which, covered as they were with frozen rain and sleet, caused such a cracking and noise as I thought I never before beard, the rattle of musketry or booming report of cannon seemed to be no comparison.

I was following in the same track and had caught up with my friend Mosley, when I discovered a light moving along the side of the train and coming towards us. Almost instantly it was opposite us, only on the bank above, we being at this time about ten feet from the train and the rebel officer, who was then peering into the car from which we had just escaped. Although the light fell full on us, so that we were plainly visible to our friends in the car, the officer did not discover us, and we remained perfectly quiet. Lieutenant Pool, however, was not so fortunate, he being the last of our party to leave the train, and had, in fact, just got off when the officer with the light came up, therefore had not examined the embankment upon which he stood, consequently dare not risk rushing over it, and as no other way of escape was possible, he was discovered, and put back into the car. Thus, our party at the outset, lost him whom each of us loved, and whose courage, daring and sound judgment, we much desired on the perilous journey we were about to commence.

A Yankee in Rebel Prisons

After seeing Lieutenant Pool comfortably stowed in the car, and kindly admonishing him that it was rather a stormy night to be out in the woods and swamps, he passed on, much to the satisfaction of Mosley and myself; and we then commenced worming our way through the unexplored briars lying between us and what we supposed an open field, but which, when we reached it, proved to be a marsh or swamp, containing an area of several acres, tufted over here and there with patches of wild grass, bullrushes and yellow willow. Soon after entering this swamp, we were greatly delighted to meet Captain Aigan, of whom we had, not seen or heard anything since we left the train. He informed us that he followed immediately after me and passed over the embankment and through the bramble thicket, close to where we did.

We were witnesses of our friend Pool's misfortune, in fact could hear the prisoners jesting him on his recapture, asking him how he stood the march? How the negroes treated him? If he found any loyal citizens? How he managed to subsist? If he was hunted down with hounds? and numerous other questions, usually asked of those who had attempted to escape, when they were brought back after being recaptured.

This, by the way, was not Pool's first attempt; he had previously made three unsuccessful efforts, and was on one occasion within hearing of the drums in our camps. Such perseverance and energy well deserved the reward of liberty, and we sincerely regretted that we were deprived of his daring and council in danger; his jovial disposition and encouragement in gloom and despondency.

After consultation we concluded to remain in the swamp, in sight of the train until it left, hoping that our friend Pool would make another effort to get away, It was nearly two hours before the engine was repaired, but during the whole of this time, although a heavy sleet continued to fall and was freezing very fast, we stood almost shoeless and half naked in the swamp, waiting and hoping for Pool to join us, and when the train moved off, we made a thorough examination of the surrounding locality, hoping to find him concealed in some clump of bushes, thinking that he had perhaps escaped a second time from the train, but dare not walk away lest he should be again discovered. Our hope and search were both in vain - he was still a prisoner.

Leaving the railroad we directed our course southward, with the intention of joining Sherman's army at Columbia, from which place we were about thirty-five miles distant. Captain Aigan had in his possession a small pocket compass, but the night was so extremely dark that it availed us nothing, and we journeyed through mud and sleet without the benefit of guide or compass, until about three o'clock next morning, when to our great joy we discovered a light in a negro hut, a short distance from the road. We carefully reconnoitered the situation, and approached near the cabin, from under which three or four savage looking hounds came barking and howling, making a noise that to us seemed sufficient to awake all creation, but our knowledge of the canine species assured us that when there was so much *bark* there was little bite, and our only fear was that they would arouse the "white folks" in the "big house," near by. Captain Aigan and myself took a position against the trunk of a large tree in front of the cabin door, while Mosley cautiously pushed open the latter and entered the interior of the negro dwelling. There was a bright, blazing fire of dry pine burning on the hearth, before which were half a dozen young negroes of both sexes, and of most any age between five and twenty years, while back in one corner of the room, raised a few feet from the floor, was a frame made of round pine poles that answered the place of a bedstead, on which was disposed a few ragged, but clean and neat looking quilts - this was the bed of the father and mother of the dusky family. No negro hut ever makes pretensions to more than one bedstead and bed, the young negroes, both male and female sleeping summer and winter on the bare floor, without clothing of any kind, except that worn by them day after day, and week after week, until literally worn off. Lieutenant M. soon aroused the old man, and informed him that three escaped Union prisoners of war were at his house, and wanted to warm themselves, and get something to eat. At the word Union the old man sprang from his bed, saying: "Massa, I'll do all I knows for you." Aigan and I were at once invited in; fresh sticks of pine were piled on the fire, in front of which, and surrounded by the young slaves, we were soon comfortably seated, thawing our limbs and drying our wet and muddy clothing.

After the firewood had burned down, and there only remained on the hearth a huge heap of red and shining embers, our host took from a sack standing by the side of his bed, a few pints of cornmeal, and in a wooden tray mixed it with cold water into a kind of dough, which he rolled up into balls, and placed them in a row on the hearth, and covered them with hot ashes and coals. We watched the operation with curiosity, as it was a new mode to us of baking bread. We thought the secret would be a great advantage to us should we be so unfortunate as to be recaptured, and taken back to prison. After about an hour had elapsed, the old man, with a long stick, commenced digging in the ashes, and to the delight of our hungry stomachs, raked out as many nice brown cakes as he had put in rolls of dough, and handed one to each of us. While we were waiting for them to cool, the old man drew a box out from under his bed, and as he did so, remarked that he had a small piece of bacon there that he had bought, and would divide with us. His master, he informed us, furnished him as much cornmeal as he could use in his family, and once a week a small ration of meat, and if he wanted more he must buy it with money earned after his daily labor for his master was completed. We found his ash-cake very good, in fact, far superior to what we had anticipated, when we saw it buried in the dirty ashes. We accordingly complimented the old fellow on his skill as a baker, which pleased him very much, and he expressed a wish that "massa Sherman would come along dat way, and he would bake a nice cake for him."

By the time we had finished our meal of ash-cake and bacon, and had got thoroughly thawed through, it was nearly daylight, which warned us that we must seek some place of safety until the shades of another night. The old man regretted very much that he could not keep us, but there was so many "white folks" on the plantation he thought we would not be safe to stay there, though he could send us to a plantation about one mile and a half distant, where we would be perfectly secure, and sent one of his boys, a young negro of about eighteen, to guide us on the route.

Arriving at the plantation, we passed by the mansion house, and filed down between two rows of negro huts to a cabin that seemed to have more pretensions to comfort than its neighbors; it was the habitation of the chief negro man, or kind of second overseer, a character that was common to almost every plantation in the South. Here, the young darkey halted us while he went in and aroused his dusky friend, to whose care we were consigned. He shortly made his appearance, and by our young guide was introduced to us as "Peter." Without hesitation he consented to conceal and feed us during the day, and conducted us off to the barn, and up into the loft, where there was an abundance of hay and fodder, and informed us that we could sleep here and be perfectly safe, adding that there was no white person on the plantation except the overseer, and he had only one arm, and consequently could not get up in the mow where we were; he then left us with the promise to return soon with something for us to eat; in the meantime we buried ourselves in the hay to sleep, and dream, perchance, of liberty, home and friends.

We enjoyed two or three hours of refreshing slumber, from which we were aroused by the voice of a man in the lower part of the barn among the stock. One of our party cautiously crawled up to the wall, and, through a chink, watched the large door below, and presently had the satisfaction of seeing the one-armed overseer come out and walk away. Two or three times during the day our friend Peter came to visit us, bringing with him, each time, something for the inner man. Peter was a genuine "business negro," and had a high appreciation of the services he was rendering us; was willing to give us a bountiful supply of corn-bread and bacon, also to keep us concealed; for anything more, he wanted to be well paid, and, as we had, at that time, a tolerable supply of rebel money, we gave him fifty dollars to bring us a roasted chicken, a dozen boiled eggs and a quart of milk, and we thought it a good bargain, as the fowl alone would have cost at least twice that amount at the sutler's shop in prison.

It was our intention to cross Broad river at Alston's ferry, twenty-five miles above Columbia, and from that point we were now eighteen miles distant, but we thought, by starting early in the evening, we could reach it before daylight next morning. Soon after dark, with Peter for a guide, we started out; he conducted us through fields, woods, and along bypaths, for about six miles, and put us on the main road leading from Winnsboro to Alston, then returned home.

In less than two hours after, we were completely lost, having taken the wrong road at the first fork we Came to after the negro left us. It being the unanimous conclusion of the whole party that we knew not where we were going, nor where we were, we resolved, the first opportunity, to press a negro guide, and soon we came to a collection of slave huts, into one of which Captain Aigan entered, while Mosley and I kept guard on the outside. Aigan soon returned, and with him a negro who assured us that he could "carry us pursisely to de road we wanted to go," Leaving all roads and following our new guide, we took an oblique direction from that we had been traveling, through fields, woods and swamps.

Two hours' travel brought us to a public highway, which the guide informed us would take us to the point before mentioned that we desired to reach; believing that we were now on the direct route and would not again lose the way that night, we took the road directed by the negro, and left him to return to his master's plantation.

It is impossible to imagine our chagrin and surprise when, two hours afterwards, we found ourselves passing over the same road and in nearly the same spot that we first discovered that we had missed the desired route. It was now getting well on in the after part of the night; we had marched hard since first starting out on the evening, and being unused to walking, were, consequently, much fatigued, especially Captain Aigan, who, having been quite unwell for several days previous to leaving the prison at Columbia, was almost completely exhausted, and seemed unable to go further; on this account, and being again bewildered in regard to the proper road, we gave up all hopes of crossing Broad river that night. But it was near daylight, and we must seek the habitation of some friendly slave for food and concealment during the approaching day, and to this end we pushed on faster than our strength would really admit. Captain Aigan was failing fast, and though we had relieved him of his haversack and blanket, was unable to walk more than a rod or two without resting, Mosley and myself kept on in advance, thinking the situation would urge him to keep in sight of us.

Traveling this way we went up a long hill on the Columbia road, and arriving at the top, we sat down to rest and wait for our friend Aigan; fifteen or twenty minutes passed, but he did not make his appearance; we were beginning to be somewhat alarmed for his safety, Mosley started down the road for the purpose of finding out what had become of him, but soon returned and reported that he had been back as far as the place we had last noticed him, but could find no trace of him; both of us then went back and carefully inspected the road, but with like success. Thinking, perhaps, he had left the road and gone over into a field on one side or the other, we went over, one on each side, and made a careful search, but in vain - he was no where to be found.

The unknown fate of our friend and companion, weighed heavily on our minds; the idea of thus abandoning one who, with ourselves, had dared the dangers of escape from the rebel guards, and shared the perils and sufferings of the nightly march through a hostile country, was abhorrent to the benevolent feelings of human nature. But, if we remained, we could render him no assistance, even if we found him, and when daylight came we would all be re-captured and consigned to a life we dreaded worse than death. It was, therefore, agreed that we should go on and seek safety for ourselves, and inform some negro of the circumstances, and have him return and look for our missing friend next day.

Going about one mile, we discovered a light burning in a negro cabin, and directed our steps thither; after reconnoitering the situation, we went up to the door and rapped; a negress came and opened it and invited us in. After being comfortably seated before the blazing pine fire, we took a survey of the interior of the building and its occupants, The old negress was engaged carding cotton, while two young girls, of about twelve and fourteen respectively, were spinning the same for cloth for their master's sons who were in the rebel army. A half a dozen young negroes of both sexes were lying heel to head and head to heel on the hearth in front of the blazing pine faggots; in the far corner of the only room the dwelling afforded, was an old dilapidated apology of a bedstead upon which were a few ragged quilts that covered the sleeping form of the "head of the family." The invariable sign (the army brass button) by which the slaves of the South distinguished Yankee soldiers, betrayed us here; this, however, gave us no uneasiness, as we never sought to conceal our character from any member of the race whose skin is black, but whose heart and head, in our great American contest remained, under all circumstances, and against all opposition, true and firm to the cause of justice and right.

When we acknowledged that we were Union soldier's, the cards and spinning wheels were put aside, and preparations commenced for our breakfast. Nearly half a peck of nice sweet potatoes were placed in a heap on the hearth, and covered with hot ashes and coals; while these were roasting, our olfactories were greeted with the rich odors of the savory slices of ham the old negress was cooking in a pan over the fire. By the time our breakfast of ham and sweet potatoes was ready, the old negro, who had been sleeping on the bedstead, came forward and took a seat in our circle; to him we made known our wish for a hiding place until night, whereupon he informed us that there was a white man lived on the adjoining plantation that was a good Union man, and had told him if he saw any Yankee soldiers that wanted assistance, to bring them to his house, and he would take care of them, and furnish them with everything in his power for their comfort. At first we hesitated whether or not to trust ourselves under the protection of a white man; had we been referred to him by any other than a negro, we certainly would not have done so, but we had too much confidence in the black man to suspect, for a moment, that he would betray us, and, accordingly, after partaking heartily of the sweet potatoes and ham, accompanied him to the residence of Mr. John Carman, the Union man referred to. Matthew was the negro's name. The surname of a slave is always the same as his master's, and changes as often as he is sold from one individual to another.

Passing outside of the inclosure surrounding Math's house, into the main road, we were startled by some one in a stifled voice calling my name. Had one of my former comrades, whose bones I had seen carried out for interment in the Georgia swamps, appeared before me, I would not have been more surprised than I was, to hear my name spoken here in a country where I supposed there was not a soul within many scores of miles with whom I had ever met. We halted, and the call was repeated; this time I answered, when, judge of the astonishment of Mosley and myself, to see our lost friend, Aigan, come out from a concealed position in a fence corner and rejoin us. Coming up the hill, where we had last seen him, exertion overcame him, and he fell exhausted and senseless to the ground, and was, it seems, lying in that position during the time Mosley and I were prosecuting the search for him, and in this condition he lay there in the mud for nearly two hours, and just recovered, and got up to the negro cabin as we were leaving it.

Our whole party now proceeded to the house of Mr. Carman. Arriving there, we remained outside, while Math went in to inform that gentleman of the charge he had brought. Mr. C., it happened, however, was not at home, but his wife, a motherly old lady (God bless her,) was possessed of the same loyal sentiments and humane feelings of her noble husband.

Their dwelling was small, and they had a great many calls and visits from their "secesh neighbors," it was not thought advisable, therefore, for us to stay in the house, so the old lady directed :Math to show us to the loom-house, an out-building on another part of the farm. Here we were made quite comfortable. Math built a big pine fire that soon threw a cheerful warmth throughout the little cabin, and soon after, Mrs. Carman, accompanied by one of her daughters, came out, bringing with them some hot tea, bread and meat, also a bundle of straw and some bed-clothing.

During the afternoon the old man arrived at home, and immediately came out to see us. In him we found one of the most zealous and loyal Union men that I have ever met either North or South; he gave us a very curious and interesting history of the early days of the rebellion in his part of the State. How their lending men pictured the future glory of the Southern States, and the ease with which an independent Confederacy could be established; and how they ridiculed the idea of any blood being shed to accomplish it.

It was our design to have moved on towards Broad river soon after dark, but Mr. C. insisted that it was best for us to remain where we were for another day at least, arguing that we had nothing to lose by lying still, while, if we moved on without knowing the situation of either our own or the rebel army, we were almost certain to be recaptured. In consideration of the wise counsel of our host, who agreed to bring us correct information in regard to the movement of the two armies, we concluded to remain until the next night in our present comfortable quarters. The cabin in which we were located was in sight, and within a few rods of, the Columbia and Winnsboro road, over which, during the night, several bodies of rebel cavalry moved towards the former place. This being known to Mr. C., who kept a vigilant watch of everything that transpired in the vicinity, he came and aroused us before daylight next morning, and informed us that we had better move out to a pine thicket on his plantation, which was farther from the road and more secluded, adding, that he feared the rebel soldiers would visit the cabin through the day in quest of forage.

The advice was good, and proved to have been very timely given, for, early in the day, a party of rebel cavalry, passing by, halted at the cabin and carried off the small bundle of fodder furnished by Mrs. Carman for the ground-work of our bed.

CHAPTER XIV

THE OLD FLAG AND LIBERTY

Two days and nights longer we remained with the kind and generous family of Mr. Carman, during which time we were the recipients of the kindest treatment and attention.

We were kept supplied with an abundance of plain, but wholesome and palatable food, furnished alternately from the tables of Mr. C. and our colored friend Math, whose larder was as well supplied as his white neighbor's, though for a slave his case was perhaps one only in ten thousand. Our clothing was also washed and repaired, and a pair of socks furnished to each of us. The old man was assiduously engaged on the road conversing with the rebel cavalry as they passed, gleaning all the information possible from them respecting the movements of the two armies, and reported accordingly to us. He and Math were both fertile in projecting and inventing schemes for our safe arrival inside the lines of the Union army.

Math's master was the owner of three fine mules, and he (Math) proposed taking these three animals and mount us on them, be taking a position behind one of us, and guide us, some dark night, to our friends, Sherman's gallant boys in blue. Math, although an original and inventive genius himself, possessed the happy faculty of coinciding with the opinions and views of everybody on every subject, and his peculiar phrase of affirmation to everything advanced, of "dats so; I knows it," was frequently the cause of an uproarious burst of hilarity from our whole party, notwithstanding our utmost efforts to keep quiet and still, lest even the rocks and pine trees should learn and prate of our whereabouts. I imagine I yet see Mosley's fat sides shaking when Math, for his invention of the plan last spoken of for our final escape, was told by one of us that he was a "first-rate fellow;" when in reply he brought into requisition his usual declaration, "dats so; I knows it."

The day before we left this hospitable family, the old gentleman came out to our concealed place in the thicket in a great hurry, and seemingly very much elated over some good news or favorable circumstances he had to communicate. Soon as his excitement had subsided and his respiration, which was almost exhausted in his anxiety to get to us, was recovered, he commenced by saying that his daughter Martha had been thinking and thinking about us, and studying how we could get through to our friends, and at last hit on the following plan:

Two of his sons were in the rebel army, and when at home on furlough had left some of their old uniform clothing, and the papers giving them authority to be absent. Martha's scheme was to dress us up in the boys' clothing, and give us forged copies of the furloughs, and start us out on the highway through the rebel lines as rebel soldiers, on leave of absence, going to our homes in Georgia.

The plan was considered feasible, and in honor to the enterprise and ingenuity of Martha, was adopted as the course we should pursue, and the old man returned to his house to make preparations accordingly. About dusk he came back, and informed us that he felt confident that it would not be necessary for us to have recourse to Martha's strategy, as our army was moving rapidly towards us, and would probably pass the next day. As convincing proof of the near approach of the Yankees, he led us out of our seclusion to an open space of ground and pointed to the red blazes of fire that illumined the horizon of the whole southwestern sky. Pointing to the chain of lights, distinguishing them by the location and different degrees of brilliancy, with an oath and exultant laugh, he would say such an one was Dr. A's residence, another Squire B's, and so on, until he had designated perhaps a dozen burning mansions, and given us the private and public history of the owner of each, with frequent interspersions to the effect that this man, or that one, was "the worst rebel and the meanest man in South Carolina, and ought to have been burned out long ago."

Notwithstanding his hate of rebels and the cause of secession, he had, as before stated, two sons in the rebel army - mere boys, the oldest not twenty years of age - but like thousands of others in the rebel armies, compelled by force to fight for a cause with which they had no sympathy. How my heart ached for the poor old mother when, with tears streaming down her furrowed cheeks, she told how they came and dragged them away from her to do battle in defense of a cause they detested. One of them was wounded and captured at the battle of Gettysburg, but was soon after exchanged, and reported that he fared better and had more care and attention shown him while a prisoner than after he returned to Richmond, and was placed in one of their own hospitals. The mother expressed an ardent desire that they might both be taken prisoners by our army, for she said they would then take the oath of allegiance to the Government of the United States, and if they fought any more it would be in the Union armies.

Early Sunday morning, February nineteenth, we could distinguish in the distance the sharp crack of musketry, and occasionally hear the booming report of the deep-mouthed cannon. As the sun rolled up toward the zenith the sound of battle became more distinct, and by moving out from our concealment to a little knoll, we could plainly see large bodies of rebel cavalry in the road and fields, about a mile distant. While watching their maneuvering, we were surprised by two of the Miss Carmans who, in great haste and breathless, made their appearance, and informed us that a wounded rebel Captain and several soldiers were at their house, and that rebel troops would probably be all over the plantation in a very short time, also adding that they had come to show us to a more secure place. We accordingly gathered up our few "traps" to follow our fair guides through swamp and thicket to the safe retreat.

Having learned in our military schooling that the tide of battle was often changed from a seeming reverse to victory, and great advantages gained by well conducted flank movements and retreats, we thought a change of base peculiarly applicable to our situation; the retrograde movement, therefore, did not in the least humble our military pride, especially as it was ordered by two fair Union damsels of South Carolina. But Captain Aigan, actuated I presume, by a desire to show his activity and agility to the young ladies - I would not at all insinuate that he was in any hurry to get away from rebel soldiers - made a dashing leap, and attempted to clear a stagnant pool of water which we had to pass around. Unlucky leap! The unfortunate Aigan, by a slip of the foot, was precipitated full length into the muddy pond. The girls turned away to conceal their mirth, while Mosley and myself give vent to an excessive outburst of laughter at the undignified position in which our friend's agility had placed him. And for the reputation of ourselves and Yankee officers generally, we sincerely advised him to make no more efforts at athletics in the presence of ladies.

The girls continued to trip lightly along, we following, and without further mishap to either of our party, we soon arrived at a dark cavernous retreat in the dense pine forest., where, as the old man afterwards remarked, "the devil himself couldn't find us." The girls returned home, leaving us crouched close to the damp ground, awaiting the issue of events.

About two hours we remained in this situation, when our fair friends again made their appearance, this, time bringing the joyful news that a squad of Union soldiers were at their house. This was indeed glad tidings, and the young girls who communicated it to us seemed to our eyes transformed into angels. We were soon threading through swamps and thickets, the same route which we had previously traveled to reach our hiding place, and as we passed by the scene of the Captain's luckless adventure on that occasion, one of the girls, with a sly wink, pertly admonished him to beware of the pond. Arriving at the family dwelling, we there found three members of the Ninety-Second Ohio Infantry - the first Union soldiers we had seen, except those that were prisoners, for nearly two years. The sight of blue-coated soldiers with guns in their hands, seemed then, to us, the most pleasing sight we ever witnessed. But our joy somewhat subsided when we learned from the soldiers that they were only a foraging party, and that the main column was moving on a road nearly twelve miles distant.

The recollection of the large body of rebel cavalry we had seen scarcely two hours before, gave us grounds to fear that we might yet be recaptured before we could reach the road upon which the troops were moving, though our friends of the Ninety-Second assured us that there was no danger, as the country between us and that point was covered with foraging parties - Sherman's bummers - as we afterwards learned to call them..

With doubts and fears, but high hopes of soon seeing the old flag, we started with our new found friends to Jeff C. Davis's Fourteenth Corps.

To this loyal family who so interested themselves in our welfare and safety, we are under lasting obligations, and the debt of gratitude we owe them can never be fully repaid. Before leaving

A Yankee in Rebel Prisons

them we drew up a certificate testifying to the kind treatment we received at their hands; also, stating that so far as we could ascertain, :Mr. Carman had always been a staunch Union man, hoping that it would be a safeguard for their property, and prevent foraging parties from Sherman's army carrying off their grain, forage and provisions.

It was about four o'clock P.M., February nineteenth, that we arrived on the banks of Broad river, and there joined the Ninety-Second Regiment Ohio Volunteer Infantry - then engaged near Alston's Ferry destroying the Columbia and Greenville rail-road.

No where in the army could we have found truer friends, or received kinder treatment, than we had at the hands of the officers and men of this noble regiment. Captain Rosser and other officers furnished us clothing, the garments we had worn in prison being ragged, dirty and infected with vermin. Lieutenant Colonel Morrow, commanding the regiment, was assiduous in his attentions, and insisted that we all board with him, but, not wishing to abuse the hospitality of the generous Colonel, we divided our patronage, and only one of us remained with his mess.

We were much surprised to learn that the army had no base of supplies or communication with the rear, and that we, consequently, would have no opportunity of getting North until a base was opened on the seaboard of North Carolina. But we were now out of the "jaws of death," and under the protecting folds of the starry flag - liberty was gained-and we could afford to bide the time between us and home and friends.

On the march with Sherman's army through the· Carolinas, we were astonished at the abundant supply of corn and bacon which the country seemed to afford. "We had so often heard the reiterated statement of rebel commissaries, that they had no meat, and could procure none for the prisoners, that, of late, we had really credited the false assertion as a fact. But Sherman's army found enough of everything necessary for the inner man to fare sumptuously every day, besides the vast quantities that were wasted and destroyed. The duty of procuring these supplies devolved on a regular detail from each regiment, called foragers, flankers, "bumers," who, according to a writer in that excellent weekly, the Army and Navy Journal, were accustomed to spread out like a great cloud of skirmishers in front of Sherman's army on its marches. These audacious gentry, who generally rode on horses and mules, borrowed of the plantations, round about, served a very good purpose as scouts. They burst over rivers, on which the enemy had established "lines of defense," and, by flanking far up or down the stream, produced, sometimes, a hasty evacuation of the works. Or, else, if Hampton's cavalry were too strong for them, they would come "piling" back, as the expressive phrase goes, to the advance of the main army, giving very good warning of what was coming. They actually "carried" certain streams and rivers where opposition was expected, and were always hanging on the skirts of the retreating rebels.

But, of course, their main demonstrations were directed upon the question of supplies, they holding to the sound doctrine that feeding an army was as important as fighting, and, by inference, their own duty in feeding was paramount to their duty in fighting.

·While the army of General Sherman was in camp at Goldsboro, North Carolina, the following humorous report was sent by the "Chief of Bummers" to Adjutant General Thomas, at Washington City:

HEADQUARTERS BUMMERS,
GRAND ARMY OF THE FLANKERS,
Goldsboro, North Carolina, April 1st, 1865.

ADJUTANT GENERAL U. S. A., WASHINGTON, D. C.:

GENERAL: I have the honor to submit the following report of the operations of my command during the Carolina campaign:

From Savannah to Columbia, in furtherance of the original plan of campaign, my forces, being poorly mounted, operated mainly upon the flanks of the Grand Army. The original plan of the campaign was for the Grand Army, after capturing Columbia, to move to the coast of Charleston.

While General Sherman was amusing his troops with experiments upon railroad iron in the vicinity of Columbia, I moved my command rapidly toward Cheraw, where I found Hardee with fifteen thousand men, strongly entrenched. Active skirmishing commenced between my mule brigade and the enemy, and I sent a courier to General Sherman apprising him of my own and the enemy's position, requesting him to set aside his original plan and move to my support, which he promptly did, and we occupied Cheraw, the enemy retreating in hasty disorder across the Great Pedee, pursued by my whole brigade. Arriving in the vicinity of Fayetteville, we met Johnston's entire army, thirty-five thousand men. We moved on the enemy strongly, driving him before us and capturing a heavy invoice of quartermasters' stores and munitions of war. From this position I sent back another dispatch requesting support. General Sherman moved his army rapidly forward; but, before he reached Fayetteville, the enemy had withdrawn across the river, and my forces were in occupation of the town.

A Yankee in Rebel Prisons

We regarded private rights, and treated the inhabitants courteously, sparing the citizens generally their houses, and, in cases of pressing want, their money and spoons.

Preparations were immediately made by General Sherman and myself for crossing the Cape Fear river with our forces, for the campaign was now so much changed from its original destination that General Sherman resolved to pursue the enemy further if possible. Having no pontoon bridge or trains with my command, it was agreed that I should cross on the bridge used by Major General Blair with his (Seventeenth) corps.

On reaching this bridge, I was notified that General Blair had directed his provost marshal to seize and confiscate the horses of my command, all of which had been borrowed by my men from loyal residents of South Carolina. Disdaining to quarrel with a provost marshal, and learning that General Blair ranked me in date of commission (by special courtesy of our excellent President towards him,) I withdrew from the bridge and effected a crossing several miles lower down, and sent notice of the same, with my compliments, to Major General Blair. I respectfully request that this uncourteous conduct on the part of General Blair be made the subject of inquiry by a military commission.

Moving forward from Fayetteville, I found Johnston strongly posted near Averysboro. Flanking his position, I crossed Black river, and advanced toward Raleigh. Near Bentonville, I found the enemy again entrenched, and again I flanked him, moving toward Goldsboro. Before reaching this town, I received a note from General Sherman requesting me to halt there, as he would be d--d if he would follow me any further.

Very Respectfully,
Your Obd't Serv't,

A Yankee in Rebel Prisons

TITUS A. BUMMER,
Commanding, etc.

The "Bummers" have really no organization, with a commander-in-chief, as the above would indicate, but each squad of from five to twenty act separately and independently, except when pressed with over whelming numbers of the enemy, when they will readily form into companies and battalions, and conduct the fight with as much order and system as a well-trained and disciplined organization. The report is, of course, the production of some humorous wag, but is notwithstanding a tolerable correct sketch of the operations of the "Bummers." Having no duty to perform, Aigan, Mosley and myself had time and opportunity of seeing and conversing with many of the citizens who remained on their plantations, along the line of march. All, with not a single exception, openly acknowledged their hostility to the Union and the Yankee army, and vowed their determination, since Sherman's march through their State, never to live in peace with the North. Their greatest grievance seemed to be the loss of the negroes. One day on the march our trio got far in the advance of the "NinetySecond," and went into a farm house to rest and chat with the ladies. The only white people living on the plantation was a young widow and her sister, an educated and accomplished young lady of about twenty. We remarked the absence of school houses in the rural districts of the South; one of them replied that they had *no use for schools* - that they employed governesses in their families while the children were small, and finished their education by sending them to boarding schools.

No interest whatever is taken by the aristocrats of the South in the education of the poor, and, as a natural consequence of the above system, they grow up almost entirely in ignorance, not one in ten being competent to write their own names. .

A Yankee in Rebel Prisons

Miss W., the younger of the two inmates of the dwelling at which we were stopping, notwithstanding the abhorrence she had for the "black, dirty-looking, Yankee soldiers, ' as she called them, favored us with several favorite airs on her piano. Her music, intelligence, and good looks, quite prepossessed our friend Mosley in her favor. The little rebel was, in fact, fast gaining his affections, but romance and love were both dashed to the ground by tbe following incident:

A staff officer coming in while the interesting tete-atete was going on, incidentally inquired where the negroes belonging to the plantation were, and was answered by the young lady that "the he ones had all done gone took to their heels, and if they came back she would shoot them." This was enough for Mosley; his admiration vanished; such language from the lips of a pretty and educated girl was more than he could endure, and before leaving he wrote on the margin of a page in a copy of "Tom Moore," 'When interrogated in regard to your negroes say they have goned and runned away.'

March fifth, the Fourteenth and Twentieth corps rested on the banks of the Great Pedee, and while here Captain Aigan visited a battery, the officers of which, he was acquainted with. From one of them he learned that Carman, our friend and protector, while making our way from captivity to freedom, was robbed of everything he possessed by a party of villainous scamps, led by a more dastardly scoundrel wearing the uniform of a United States officer. When they approached the house on their thieving mission the old lady protested against their taking all - was willing to share - and informed the party that they were and always had been Union people - also showed them the certificate we had given them, testifying to their care and kind treatment of us. But this availed nothing, as the contemptible puppy calling himself an officer, shamefully abused her, saying that it was a bogus thing they had got up themselves, and that there were no such officers in the army. These facts we learned from the officers of the battery before mentioned, one of whom, the day following, with a squad of men, visited the plantation. When the circumstances were related to him, he asked to see the paper we left them; glancing over it, he recognized in Oaptain Aigan's name an old friend, and felt it his duty to render all the assistance in his power to those who had so kindly protected him, and communicated the facts to his men, who immediately made up a considerable amount of money and donated it to the destitute but generous family, who, in prosperity, had so materially aided the escape of Union prisoners of war to freedom and friends.

On the eleventh of March, Sherman's whole army entered Fayetteville, North Carolina, having been on the campaign fifty-four days - twenty-five of which we had marched with it. We were rejoiced to learn that communication would be opened from here with Wilmington, and we would consequently have an opportunity of going Northward. The next day Captain Ainsworth reached Fayetteville from Wilmington on a tug, up the Cape Fear river, one hundred and twenty miles, spite of the reports current that the river was filled with torpedoes, and blocked up by trees, and by the rebel ram *Chickamauga* sunk across it, and that numerous rebel batteries were established at different points on the river. He made the trip up with entire safety, without losing a man, although continually fired into by the rebels along the shore. We were kindly furnished transportation on this craft, and the afternoon of the day following we bid farewell to our generous friends of the Ninety-Second, and sailed for the city of Wilmington, and from thence proceeded to Washing-ton - got our "greenbacks "- and went on our several ways, rejoicing that gloomy prison walls no longer surrounded us - that we were free to breathe the fresh, pure air of heaven, and experience once more the endearing influence of home and friends, beneath the protecting folds of the "starry banner. "

CHAPTER XV

While in Charleston, confined in the work house, there one day filed by that building about one thousand of the most wretched, pitiable, and abject looking human beings that in any land – christian, heathen or pagan - ever trod the Almighty's footstool, or breathed the air of heaven. Black as most of the slaves on any plantation in the "Confederacy," gaunt, haggard and thin as skeletons, and the Kickapoo Indian, clad in his breach-clout, leggings and moccasins, is magnificently and comfortably costumed in comparison with these poor wretches. In surprise and horror you ask who they were? *United States soldiers,* whom the fortunes of war had thrown into the hands of a people, who, with many appeals to Christian principles, asked the favor of Divine Providence on the cause in which they were engaged, but as a just retribution of their wicked deeds, the Almighty cursed them instead. These poor victims of their fiendish treatment were fresh from the prison hell at Andersonville, Georgia. We had previously heard much of the horrors of that detestable place, but never before had we beheld any of the unfortunates whose fate it was to be there confined, and we were now convinced that imagination failed to picture their misery. At Wilmington we again came in contact with several hundred of these hapless victims of rebel barbarity. The testimony of these men relative to the cruelties practiced on them by rebel officials is too horrible for civilized people to contemplate, and many of them too, when giving it, were in the last agonies of death. It is true the class of prisoners we met here were the worst cases, such as were not able for removal to more northern hospitals; but the treatment of all was the same, and those possessing the greatest powers of endurance were of course the least afflicted.

While in Wilmington I visited the various hospitals in which our men who had been prisoners were receiving medical treatment.

One of the surgeons in charge informed me that there were nearly three hundred cases under treatment, all of whom would lose either one or both feet, in consequence of *cold, exposure, and scurvy.* Amputation was not necessary, as they had so rotted that a pair of scissors was only required to clip the sinews, which left the bone sometimes protruding several inches beyond the putrid and decaying flesh.

Concerning the general condition of the prisoners arriving at Wilmington, Doctor J. C. Dalton, professor of Physiology and Microscopic Anatomy, in the College of Physicians and Surgeons, in the city of New York, made the following report:

"The better cases were walking about the streets, perhaps barefooted, or with no other clothing than a pair of white cotton drawers and an old blanket or over-coat, both equally ragged. In these, the slow, dragging gait, listless manner and cavernous, inexpressive look of the face, together with the general emaciation, formed a peculiar aspect, by which they alone attracted the attention of the passer-by, and by which they were at once distinguished from the other convalescent soldiers. There was no occasion to inquire in Wilmington which were our returned prisoners; after half a day's experience anyone could distinguish them at a glance. Many of them, who had strength to crawl about in this manner, were prevented from doing so by the want of clothing. Major Randlete, the Provost Marshal of Wilmington, told me that on one day forty of these men came into our lines absolutely as naked as they were born. I inquired of a considerable number of them, whom I saw in the hospitals confined to their beds, naked, or with only a shirt, and covered with a hospital blanket, what had become of their clothing, and was told that they had thrown away what remained as soon as they could obtain shelter, because it was so ragged, filthy, and full of vermin. One of them, on being told that the Sanitary Commission had sent them flannel shirts and drawers, caught at the words with a childish eagerness, and repeated the good news to his companions with a faint, half-imbecile smile, as long as I was within hearing. With the great majority of the feebler ones personal cleanliness was a thing which they appeared to have entirely forgotten. They no longer retained sufficient strength, either of mind or body, to appreciate or correct the degradation to which months of unavoidable filthiness had reduced them. In the most extreme cases the condition of the mind, as well as the expression of the face, was absolutely fatuous, and the aspect of the patient was not that of a strong man reduced by illness, but that of an idiotic pauper, who had been such from his birth. Nevertheless, several of the surgeons informed me that the condition of the patients had visibly improved since their reception, and that I could not then form an adequate idea. of what it was when they entered our lines. In that case it must have been lamentable beyond description.

The testimony of both men and officers was uniform as to the causes of their unnatural condition. These causes were, first, starvation, and second, exposure. Only such officers and men as could procure money were able to obtain anything like sufficient nourishment. Some of them told me that during the entire winter they had received absolutely no meat; a pint of corn-meal, often with the cob ground-in, sometimes with and sometimes without salt, a handful of "cowpeas," and sometimes sorghum molasses, constituted their usual ration. When in hospital, they had only very thin corn-meal gruel and a little corn bread. To the debility occasioned by this insufficient food was added that resulting from exposure. It was a common thing for a prisoner, immediately on being taken, to be stripped of his clothing - shoes, socks, pantaloons, shirts and drawers - and to be left with only an old worn out pair of drawers, and perhaps an equally worn out shirt and blanket given him in exchange. This robbery of clothing was also practiced more or less on officers. Even an assistant surgeon, who was captured within four miles of Richmond, told me that he was robbed of his flannel shirt while standing in front of Libby Prison, and in presence of the rebel officer in charge of the squad. This was immediately after his arrival in the city, and when he had been, for the three days succeeding his capture, entirely without food. With the scanty clothing thus left them, the men were kept during the winter, often without any shelter, excepting such as they could contrive to provide by excavating a sort of rifle-pit in the ground, and covering it with old blankets and canvass, as their supply of fuel was insufficient, and sometimes entirely wanting. Even in the hospitals their suffering from cold was very great.

One of the most melancholy sights in Wilmington, was that to be seen at the 'Geer' hospitals. In these hospitals were collected all those patients who had lost their feet, either wholly or in part, by freezing, from their exposure during the past winter, and this in a well-wooded country. In some of them two or three toes only, on one or both feet, were gangrened, and in process of separating by ulceration; in others both feet had entirely separated, and the patients were awaiting the time when their general strength and the condition of the stump would warrant a final amputation, In many cases the patients ascribed this gangrene directly to frost-bites received on particular occasions; in others to their illness from which they were suffering - generally fever combined with exposure. My own impression, derived from the result of many inquiries, was, that it was generally due to a continuous depression of the vital energies from starvation and neglect, resulting gradually in .a destruction of the life of those parts most exposed to the cold and the weather.

The only wonder is, that so many survived the brutalities to which they were subjected by those fiendish monsters, General

A Yankee in Rebel Prisons

John H. Winder, Captain Henry Wertz, and other inhuman and merciless rebel officials, and not that so large a number perished. To say that the Southern people, as a mass, were responsible for these outrages on humanity and christian civilization, would be an unjust aspersion, for there were among them many kind and sympathizing hearts who would gladly have exerted themselves to mitigate as far as possible the sufferings of the unfortunate prisoners, had they been allowed that privilege, by the officials whom Jeff Davis, in consideration of their cruel natures, appointed ostensibly for the purpose of taking care of prisoners of war, but really to murder them. Had these cruelties been the result of accident instead of a deliberate purpose to totally incapacitate our soldiers for future service, more leniency might be shown the ex-President of the rebel States, and the minions who executed his hellish designs. But in Georgia, Alabama, and even in the Carolinas, our troops found everywhere an abundance of corn and bacon, which could well have been shipped to Andersonville, or any other point where our men were confined, as the capacity of the roads in these localities for transportation, was not over-taxed, as they were in the immediate vicinity of the rebel armies, where, if our men had been confined there, there might have been some apology for short rations; and, further, it was always in their power to confine their prisoners in healthy localities, and provide them with comfortable quarters, had they been so disposed to do, instead of sending them into the miasmatic swamps of Georgia, and then herding thirty-five thousand on an area of less than thirty acres.

Colonel Ould, under date of March seventeenth, 1863, in a communication to his master, exulting over the complete success of the wicked scheme to destroy Union prisoners, says:

A Yankee in Rebel Prisons

"The arrangements I have made (for exchanging prisoners) works largely in our favor. We get rid of a set of miserable wretches and receive some of the best material I ever saw."

A portion of the rebel Congress once visited Mr. Davis, to remonstrate against the treatment of Union prisoners, but their petition was refused by Davis and his cabinet, on the ground of policy merely. A rebel Lieutenant connected with the guard at Andersonville prison, who still possessed some principles of humanity, once remonstrated with General Winder on the general barbarous treatment of the prisoners, and suggested a plan for furnishing them with a sufficient quantity of sweet and healthy water, adding that hundreds were dying solely on account of not having good water. The hoary headed old traitor flew into a violent passion and replied," the G-d d--d wretches are not dying half fast enough."

One of the prisoners confined in this Golgotha, in an excellent article in the Atlantic Monthly, describes as follows the appearance and condition of the old prisoners in the Andersonville *pen* when he entered that hopeless receptacle of Union prisoners:

"There were at this time under torture, twenty-eight thousand prisoners, and as the Southern Confederacy, a christian association, and conducting itself with many appeals to christian principle, believes "the wind is tempered to the shorn lamb," and so shears the Yankees as close as possible. These men had been formerly fleeced of such worldly gear as blankets, money and clothing. Some further shearing there had been also, but irregular, depending chiefly on the temper of the captors, stripping them sometimes to shirt and drawers, leaving them occasionally jacket and shoes; so now most were barefooted, most in rags, and some had not even rags. They had lain on the bare earth, sodden with damp or calcined into dust, and borne storm and heat helplessly, without even the shelter of a board, until they were burned and wasted to the likeness of haggard ghosts. Most had forgotten hope, many decency; some were dying, and crawled over the ground with a woeful persistency that it would have broken your heart to see. They were all fasting, for the day's rations, tossed to them the afternoon before, had been devoured, as was the custom, at a single meal, and proved scant at that; and they crowded wolfishly about the wagons, the most miserable, pitiable mob that ever had mothers, wives and sisters at home to pray for them."

The rations drawn - the same writer goes on to describe their quantity, and quality and their manner of preparing them to be eaten. He says:

"A day's rations, remember, were eight ounces of Indian meal, cob and kernel ground together, (as with us for pigs) and sour, (a common occurrence) and two ounces of condemned pork. Salt was not even hinted at, the market price of that article being four dollars a pound at Andersonville. Eight ounces of meal, made a cake six inches long, five broad, and half an inch thick." That is to say, three meals were comprised in a mass six inches long, five broad, and half an inch thick; but the famished prisoners generally preferred taking the three meals in one, and even then their hungry stomachs were not satisfied; yet they got no more until the same hour next day. Their rations devoured, as the shades of night approach, the prisoners go to bed, which he say's was, "quite an elaborate arrangement as practiced among us, what with taking off our clothes, and possibly washing and combing, and pulling up of sheets and coverlets, and fitting of pillows to neck and shoulders; but nothing can be more simple than the way they do it there. You just lie down wherever you are - and sleep - if you can."

A Yankee in Rebel Prisons

Referring to the general debility of the prisoners, and the horrible, sickening, and offensive condition of the camp or prison pen, he speaks as follows:

"Stomach and body weakened by a perpetual hunger, and, in many cases, utter inability to retain food, good or bad. More than that, the sluggish water course that served as their reservoir crept across their pen foul and thick with the *debris* of the rebel camp above, and in the center filtered through the spongy ground, and creamed and mantled and spread out loathsomely in a hateful swamp; and the fierce sun, beating down on its slimy surface, drew from its festering pools and mounds of refuse, a vapor of death, and the prisoners breathed it; and the reek of unwashed and diseased bodies, crowding close on each other, and the sickening, pestilential odor of a huge camp without sewerage or system of policing, made the air a horror, and the prisoners breathed it."

The treatment received by our prisoners at the hands of southern rebels, although presented to the public, in the papers of the day, has never been portrayed in colors sufficiently vivid, and the fiendish natures of those men, appointed by Jeff Davis, to kill them by inches, to torture them to death, never have, and never can be set forth in words. In fact, language is incapable of conveying the horrors of the sufferings of Union soldiers who were confined on Belle Isle, at Andersonville, Millen, Florence and Saulsbury.

CHAPTER XVI

EIGHT MONTHS IN THE PEN

Henry M. Roach, private of Company G, Seventy-Eighth regiment Ohio volunteers, was captured on the Atlanta campaign, and near that city; from his statements I derive some interesting particulars. He was marched on the -------- day of September, along with other prisoners, to the pen at Andersonville – a huge, roofless inclosure, made of squared pines set perpendicularly and close together in the ground. As they butted up against it, their eyes were greeted by sight of about fifty dead bodies deposited in rows on either side of the gate, which, as they entered, should have wailed forth, "*Leave all hope behind.*"

For two months, he .says, they never tasted bread, having learned by experience that a half pint of Indian meal would go farther towards "filling up" when made into gruel than if baked in the ashes, or on a chip in front of the smoky, pine fire. In fact, they eat everything issued them, either raw, or boiled. Beans, meal, rice, and the microscopic bulk of rancid bacon, were all boiled together, and devoured at one meal. The water which they used was procured from a small stagnant stream that coursed through the center of the camp, and served the double purpose of furnishing water for cooking, drinking, and washing, and as a sewerage for the filth and refuse matter accumulated on the ground on which there lived thirty thousand hopeless men. As a consequence, all suffered, and many sickened and died from the daily use of the impure and poisonous liquid. But their sufferings from this cause were at length alleviated, by (what the prisoners believed) a merciful intervention of Providence. From one of the most elevated portions of the prison grounds, and which had always been perfectly dry, excepting when it rained very heavily, there suddenly, and without any previous signs, burst forth a fountain, thick as a man's arm, of pure, sweet and healthy water, and during the time the prisoners remained there, it continued to flow, without any abatement, as full and strong a current as when it first spouted up from the bowels of the earth.

They were robbed of everything that could, in the smallest degree, contribute to the health or comfort of either man or beast, neither clothing, blankets or shelter of any kind was allowed them, nor scarcely fuel sufficient to cook their starvation ration of Indian meal, (this, too, in the midst of a country abounding in great forests of huge pine timber) to say nothing of an amount necessary to preserve the warmth of life in naked human beings, exposed, as they were, day and night, to the inclemency of an unfriendly latitude in mid winter. Through the day, when the sun would come out for a little while, and lend his kindly smiles to the encouragement of the poor prisoners, they would huddle together, and, in heaps, on the ground, endeavor to sleep. But when night, with its chilly dews and poisonous vapors, enveloped the camp, they might have been seen in squads of fifteen and twenty, crouched together over the suffocating smoke of a few green pine faggots, which, occasionally, by dint of hard blowing, sent up for a moment a cheerful blaze. Thus most of them sat and watched, and cursed, and prayed night after night, throughout the long, dreary, wretched winter. Others, however, whom cold and starvation had not reduced so greatly in strength and energy, would keep on their feet, and pace up and down the camp all night. This, also, to prevent perishing with the cold and frost.

TRADING DEAD MEN FOR WOOD

To such a famishing, freezing condition were the poor, miserable wretches at Andersonville brought by the constant, systematic cruelty and deprivation to which they had been subjected by

A Yankee in Rebel Prisons

the officials having them in charge, that it might almost literally be said that they resorted to the plan indicated by the above heading, to procure a. few slender sticks of fuel, with which to cook their coarse, unbolted meal, and to keep heat in their bodies, and their extremities from absolutely freezing. The phrase, "Trading dead men for wood," originated in this way : - when a prisoner died, two or three of his comrades, some time during the next twenty-four hours succeeding the event, were allowed to carry him outside of the stockade, which gave them an opportunity of picking up a few sticks of wood as they returned.

It is impossible to realize the terrible condition, both of body and mind, that human beings - men, naturally of noble and generous impulses - are brought to, when they absolutely *rejoice* at such occasions as the above, for the opportunity of procuring a few chips or splinters of green fuel. .

When Sherman started on the march southward from Atlanta, in October, 1864, most of the prisoners were removed from Andersonville to Savannah, Millen, and other points, which, it was thought, would be beyond the reach of our armies. And during the whole time (three days) occupied in the removal, not one morsel of food was furnished, and the fourth day they only received three small crackers. "The first day of our fasting (says my brother, from whom I derive the information), we were hungry, *very* hungry; the second day, we seemed to have overcome it and did not suffer so much, but the third day, even the most hale and stout of us were absolutely so weak that it was impossible to maintain an erect position but for a few minutes at a time." .

Human nature shudders at the bare recital of the atrocities practiced by the incarnate fiends in charge of the southern prisons on the unfortunate victims who filled them. Hundreds of them were reduced by starvation and brutal treatment to such a degree of wretchedness, that they deliberately walked up to the "dead line," that the guards might shoot them, and thus end their misery. "Two hundred and sixty-seven of these cases," writes Miss Clara Barton, from Andersonville, whither she had went on a mission of love and philanthropy, "were disinterred in one day for decent burial."

Let those who think the statements that have, from time to time appeared in the public prints, are the sensation articles of hired correspondents, or exaggerated testimony of our returned prisoners, suffering (as they think) imaginary wrongs, read the following letter, written by a Georgia planter, who resided in the vicinity of Andersonville, while our prisoners were confined there, and who, consequently, had an opportunity of knowing the spirit hat animated the officials connected with that Golgotha, and the condition of the hapless victims of their cruelty:

"NEW YORK, *Thursday, August 3d.*
"To the Editors of the Evening Post:

"There appears to be a disposition on the part of some of the public press to mitigate the offenses and crimes of Major Henry Wertz, late the responsible keeper of the stockade at Andersonville, Georgia, and to throw upon others the responsibilities that justly attach to those alone who were in immediate command of that prison. Being personally acquainted with most of the officers who were stationed at Andersonville, and knowing much of the treatment of those who were so unfortunate as to have been confined in that pen of horror, I have thought that a condensed statement of how things were managed, and prisoners of war treated there, might not be entirely unacceptable to your readers.

I wish to be understood as not desirous to forestall the action or opinion of the commission which is about to investigate this matter, or to add anything to the feeling entertained toward Major Wertz. It is enough for him to rest, now and forever, under an obloquy that no time and no repentance can obliterate; to feel within himself the unenviable pangs which the recollection of his powerless murdered victims will ever arouse, and to know that whatever may be the award of a human tribunal, his punishment is already decreed.

The prison of Andersonville is a stockade about eighteen feet high, the posts comprising it being sunk in the ground five feet; it originally comprised an area of eighteen acres, but was subsequently enlarged to twenty-seven acres. The inclosure is upon the side of a hill, looking toward the south, at the foot of which is a small brook about five feet wide and as many inches deep, which furnished the water for the use of the prisoners. Within this inclosure were turned the prisoners as they arrived, and left to provide for themselves, there being no shelters, or arbors, or any kind of protection afforded by trees or otherwise against the burning rays of the Southern sun, the furious storms or the freezing winters.

The position was selected by Captain Winder, a son of General John H. Winder, who was sent from Richmond for that purpose in the latter part of 1868. When it was suggested to him by a disinterested, but humane spectator, of his operations, that it would, perhaps, be better to leave the trees standing within the Proposed stockade, as they would afford shade to the prisoners, he replied: 'That was just what he was not going to do; he was going to make a pen for the Yankees, where they could rot faster than they could be sent there.' And admirably did he accomplish his mission.

The first commandant of the post was Colonel Persons, who was soon succeeded by John H. Winder, with his son as Adjutant, his nephew as Commissary and Sutler, and Henry Wertz in immediate command of the prisoners. There were generally stationed there, for guard duty, from three to six regiments of infantry, with one company of artillery, having a battery of six pieces; according to the exigencies of the case, the number of prisoners then confined, or the fears entertained of an attempt to set them at liberty by raiding parties of United States troops.

When prisoners were first received, it was usual to subject them to a search for money, valuables, etc., which, ostensibly were to be restored, when they were released from captivity, but which, in reality, went into the pockets of those who controlled the prison. Notwithstanding a law of the Confederacy expressly prohibiting the dealing in 'greenbacks,' yet the initiated, a few whose 'loyalty' was unquestioned, could always obtain, for a consideration, the greenbacks they required.

The writer of this was the foreman of the last grand jury which was impaneled for Sumner county, Georgia, and, in the performance of his duties, he had to investigate a large number of presentments for dealing in the forbidden currency, which was brought against poor Union men in every instance. Struck by this fact, he resolved to examine, as his position gave him a right to do, into all the circumstances: where money originally came from, who did the selling of it, indeed the whole *modus operandi,* and he elicited the fact above stated, how the money was obtained, that the Winders and Wertz were the principals, acting through subordinates, in gathering bushels of plums, in the way of premiums, etc. Meanwhile the prisoners were left to the tender mercies of their jailor and commissary for their food, which might have been improved in quantity at least, if their money had been left in their own possession.

A Yankee in Rebel Prisons

At first it was customary to send a wagon into the stockade every morning at ten o'clock, loaded with the rations for the morning – bacon and corn bread, nothing else; but as the number of prisoners increased and the greed of gain grew upon the trio above mentioned, the corn bread was reduced in its quality, being then manufactured of equal proportions of ground field peas and corn, unbolted, unsifted, uncleansed, indeed, from the trash which peas naturally accumulate; and, at last, when the number of prisoners increased to over thirty-seven thousand, the meat rations per week were reduced to a piece of bacon, for each man, about three inches long and two wide, with one pone of the bread above described per day. Then, also, the custom of carrying the prisoners' food into the stockade was abolished. They drove up to the gates, which were slightly opened, and the scanty food, foul and unhealthy as it was, was thrown inside by the guard, to be scrambled for by the wretched prisoners, the strongest and those nearest the gate getting the largest share, the weak and sickly getting none.

I have mentioned the small brook which runs through the lower part of the stockade, and which supplied the water for drinking and washing. This brook has its rise in a swamp not far from the prison, and at no time, certainly not a lengthened period, was the water suitable or healthy; but when the feces and filth, the drainage of the whole camp of prisoners, came to be superadded to the natural unfitness of the water for drinking or cleansing purposes, my readers can judge what thirst was assuaged, or fever cooled, or throbbing temples washed, by this floating stream of filth and disease! At any time, under the most rigid hygienic restrictions, it is difficult to maintain health and cleanliness among a large body of men - what do you think was the condition of thirty-seven thousand half-naked, half-starved men, without any police regulations, under no moral or restraining influences? If the remnant who were finally allowed to pass out of this military Golgotha were not wild beasts, unwashed, befouled devils, no thanks are to be given to Henry Wertz for lack of effort to produce such a consummation.

When it rained, as it does in that climate almost continually during the spring and fall months, the soil within the inclosure was one mass of loblolly, soft mud, at least fifteen inches in depth, through which stalked and staggered the gaunt, half-clad wretches thus confined. *The stench from the prison could be perceived for two miles, and farmers living in the neighborhood began to fear for the health of their families.*

As a consequence of this, the hospitals – facetious was Wertz in his horrible humanity - were crowded to repletion with the emaciated, starved and diseased men who were trundled into them.

The hospitals were constructed of logs, unhewed, the interstices unfilled and open, admitting the rain, without floors, cots, bunks or blankets, filthy and fetid with the festering, putrid bodies of the sick, the dying and the dead. Words fail, language is impotent to describe one of these dens of disease and death. I once mustered the courage, impelled by the earnest entreaties of a Northern friend, to enter one of them, to visit one who was tenderly reared, and walked in the best ranks of Connecticut society. I believed I had seen before this what I deemed to be human wretchedness in its worst forms. I thought that I could nerve myself to witness mortal agony and wretchedness, and destitution, as I had heard it described, without blanching or trembling. But if the condensed horrors of a hundred 'black holes' had been brought before my mind to prepare me for the ordeal, they would have failed to realize the facts as I saw them face to face.

A Yankee in Rebel Prisons

.   I cannot, in a daily paper, read by innocence and virtue, detail what met my sight on the occasion I refer to. I will not pollute any page, save the records of the courts that must try the culprit for the crime of torture by disease and filth, with the details of that caravansary of horrible, intentional slaughter. For fear that some may think I have exaggerated, an episode here will, perhaps, dispel such illusion. Convicted by the horrible fact that was a stench in his nostrils, General Winder, then Commissary General of Prisons, but having his headquarters at Andersonville, was forced by decency, not humanity, for this he himself asserted, to ask the aid of the Presiding Elder of the Methodist Church of that circuit.to adopt some means to alleviate the miseries and soothe the wretchedness of the poor inmates of that Andersonville hospital. This gentleman invoked the co-operation of the women of Sumter county, who responded with clothing and necessaries only, for these alone are allowed, to the amount of four wagon loads. Upon the day appointed, four ladies, accompanied by their husbands, went to the prison and sought from the Provost Marshal a pass, to take their benefactions to the sick prisoners. It was refused with a curse! The party proceeded to Winder's headquarters, where Henry Wertz \vas in company with the General. The demand for a pass was repeated. Understand, the ladies were present, and the reasons given why the party were there, in accordance with Winder's special request. To their astonishment they were met with this reply: 'G-d d--n you, have you all turned Yankees here?'

'No, General,' responded the spokesman of the party, 'I am not, as you know, nor are any here present; we have come, as you requested us, through Rev. Mr. D., to bring necessary articles for the Federal hospital, and ask a pass for the purpose of delivering them.'

'It's a d--d lie! I never gave permission for anything of the kind! Be off with you, all of you!'

As if this fearless display of martial valor and gentlemanly bearing was not sufficient, Henry Wertz essayed to and did eclipse his General in profanity and indecency; and I here assert that if the lowest sinks of the most abandoned parts of your city were gleaned, they could not surpass the ribald vulgarity and finished profanity of this jailor, exhibited in the presence of refined and 'loyal' ladies.

Shocked, terrified, beaten to the very dust with mortification, the party retired, and, foiled in their efforts to succor the sick, or alleviate the tortures of the dying Union soldier, they gave their loads of clothing and food to a passing column of Federal soldiers on their way to another place -:Millen. They at least had the satisfaction of knowing that some were benefitted even if they had failed in their efforts for those who most needed their assistance.

During the last winter - which was unusually cold for Georgia, when the ice made an inch thick - no shelter, no blankets or clothes, no wood was provided for the wretched inmates of that prison. Squads were permitted, to the number of thirty, to go out under guard daily for one hour, without axes or any cutting tool, to gather the refuse and rotten wood in the forests; and if they outstayed their time they were tried by a drumhead court martial, charged with violating their parole, and, if found guilty, were hung. I, myself, saw three bodies hanging who were thus executed. Poor fellows, I thought, God has taken pity upon you and given you deliverance from your cruel jailor. When you and I meet, at another judgment seat, woe to him if his authority be found insufficient for the taking of your lives, wretched though they be.

My house was the resort - or I should say refuge of most of the prisoners who made their escape from the stockade, and the tales of starvation and distress which they told would have melted an iron heart. I must close my hurried account of what I had seen. It is far from full; not one half has been told; by far the most has been kept back from very shame, and in respect to your readers. I have not embellished. The pictures were too rough, the characters too forlorn for the flowers of rhetoric to bloom in their presence. Broken hearts, crushed spirits and. manhood trampled on, may answer as fitting subjects for the romancer's pen, but the horrible reality, so seldom seen, burns its images upon the beholder's soul, that no other impressions can efface, and they remain life-pictures indeed."

But facts and statements, and the sworn testimony of returned prisoners, have already enough been adduced to fasten forever the scorn of the civilized world upon the inhuman perpetrators of these fiendish deeds. And so long as they go unpunished, the wail

of ten thousand widowed wives and orphaned children will shriek along the western prairies, among New England hills, upon the shores of the lakes, and upon the sea coast, crying aloud for vengeance.

CHAPTER XVII

PERSONAL SKETCHES

It was the intention to drop here the trail of the history, so briefly and imperfectly sketched, of the most trying vicissitudes and sufferings that any soldiers of the Union armies experienced during the gigantic war to crush the great rebellion of the Southern slave holders. But it would be recreant to the trust of friendship, and callous to the holy inspirations that chord with the genius of old associations, did I omit mention of the names of those brave and gallant comrades Major B. C. G. Reed, Lieutenant E. N. Read, Major (now Brevet Brigadier General) Harry White, and other noble spirits with whom I was associated during the long, dark period of our imprisonment.

MAJOR HARRY WHITE

One of the most popular officers, generous friends, and gallant soldiers, confined with me in the Libby and other rebel prisons was Major (now Brevet Brigadier General) Harry White. He was captured at Winchester, Virginia, in June, 1863, his regiment, the Sixty-Seventh Pennsylvania, of which he was then in command, being left there, with two or three others, to cover the evacuation and retreat of Major General Milroy's main army, when compelled to abandon that point by an overwhelming force of the rebels under Lieutenant General Ewell, the fifteenth of June, 1863.

Major White, by his noble qualities of head and heart, soon endeared himself to his associates in prison. An earnest, eloquent, and fearless speaker, he took a prominent part in all efforts of the prisoners to make our suffering condition known to our friends in the North - to condemn the brutal atrocities of the rebel authorities - and to stigmatize with just condemnation the base conduct of those among us, who, with rebel hearts, but wearing the United States uniform endeavored to stifle the voice of our reasonable complaints, thereby sanctioning the action of rebels, and misleading our government and friends at home.

Major, while with us in Libby, was also ye editor of the "Libby Chronicle," a journal devoted to politics and religion, and chronicler of events in prison life. It was written on foolscap, and read weekly to the assembled : "Libbyites."

Efforts were made during the fall of 1863, by the Major's friends in Pennsylvania, to have him released by a special exchange, and as he was at that time a member of the Pennsylvania State Senate, the vote of which was a tie, without his ballot, which would be cast with the Union side, our commissioner for exchange of prisoners readily assented, and proposed to Robert Ould, rebel commissioner, to exchange for Major White any Confederate officer, of the same rank, whom our government held a prisoner of war. But the rebel officials, hoping to retard and confuse the organization of the Pennsylvania Legislature, which, with White present, was Republican, or Union, by the majority of one, would not consent to give him up, thinking, no doubt, they thereby materially aided the enemies of the Union in the Keystone State; who, it is reasonable to suppose, were thankful for the favor.

In November all the Surgeons confined in Libby Prison, some of whom had been prisoners for many months, were exchanged and sent North. When they were called out of the prison, Major White stepped into their ranks and passed out as one of the disciples of Esculapius. Not either the officials connected with the prison, or those who conducted the prisoners to City Point, were aware that a Yankee Major was in the party. The fact, however, was known to many of the prisoners, and one whose name appears in another chapter of this volume in no enviable light, was soon after in close consultation with Major Turner, commandant of the prison, and nearly all the prisoners were of the opinion that he communicated the information concerning the Major's exit from the prison, to that worthy, who telegraphed the fact to City Point, and he was accordingly taken back to Richmond.

Soon after this attempt to escape, he was taken from Libby to Salisbury, and for some time kept handironed and in solitary confinement. No reason was ever assigned for this outrageous proceeding. But the natural inference of those who had daily opportunities of witnessing the malicious conduct of rebel officials, was that they wished to torture and pile indignities on him on account of his prominent Republican proclivities.

In the following spring he was taken out of the prison at Salisbury, and started en route for Macon, where most of the Union officers, prisoners of war, were then confined. He escaped from the guard on the route, and succeeded in getting far into the mountains of western North Carolina, where he was tracked by the dogs, and finally recaptured. When, a few days subsequent, he was turned in the stockade with us at Macon, many of his former friends absolutely wept on beholding his torn and mangled body. Arms, legs and shoulders bore great gashes - tooth-prints of the savage dogs with which their more savage masters trailed and captured him.

From this time until exchanged, in the following September, he was kept with, and on the same footing as the other prisoners, on whom his straight forward, manly character, affable disposition, patience and endurance under all circumstances, exercised a cheerful and genial influence.

A Yankee in Rebel Prisons

DRISCOLL AND PAVEY

Among the many noble victims of rebel persecution and barbarity, none had such extensive and bitter experience of that refined mode of torture - solitary confinement on coarse and insufficient food, in dank, dark, underground dungeons - as Captain E. M. Driscoll, Third Ohio Volunteers, and Lieutenant C. W. Pavey, Eightieth regiment Illinois Infantry. By their fearless and out spoken opinions in regard to the "Confederacy," and the leaders thereof, they each rendered themselves peculiarly obnoxious to rebel officials, which resulted in their being taken without form or ceremony and confined in damp, narrow cells, and informed that they were to be executed in retaliation for the death of two rebel recruiting officers, executed for violation of a standing order issued by Major General Burnside, while in command of the Department of the Ohio.

In torture and agony, both of body and mind, these officers were confined in the dark, damp, filthy dungeon described in a former chapter of this volume, *one hundred and forty-seven days*. Nearly every day they were visited by Dick Turner, who, with curses and abusive epithets, would taunt and insult them in the most shameful manner.

Their rations most of the time consisted exclusively of about one-half pound of coarse corn bread per day for each of them, with a sufficient quantity of James river water, to "wash it down." Nor were they allowed the privilege of communicating with their friends, or any parties outside of the prison; and their hopes and fears were alternately excited by such information as the keepers of the prison choose to give them. One day they would be informed that the authorities had fully determined on their execution, and they had as well make preparation for that interesting occasion, while, perhaps, the very next day they would be informed by the same authority that all hostages were to be released, and they would accordingly be exchanged immediately. Thus passed their time through all these wretched, dreary days, weeks, and months, their cruel tormentors inspiring them with hope one day merely for the satisfaction of dashing it to the ground the next, leaving them more depressed in spirits and physical energy than at first. .

Imprisonment, even under the most favorable circumstances, with a sufficient quantity of wholesome and palatable food, pure water, comfortable beds, and light, airy rooms, with opportunities for exercising, is, indeed, a most wretched state of existence; but imagination can not realize the sufferings and misery of those, who, like Captain Driscoll and Lieutenant Pavey, for nearly five months were shut out from the pure air of heaven and the sun's cheerful rays, in a wretched, cave-like dungeon beneath the surface of the earth, and whose slimy walls sent forth a pestilential odor, from which there was no escape. But their brave hearts and good constitutions survived the cowardly attempt to murder them by inches, and they lived to return to their friends and liberty, though with wasted frames and health permanently impaired.

SIGMOND COUNT VON BRAIDAY

This gentleman was many months a prisoner, and shared with us the hardships and deprivations of our confinement at Macon, Charleston and Columbia, and by his gentlemanly conduct, courteous manners, and soldierly bearing, endeared himself to all. . He is the second son of an Austrian nobleman, and is himself a native of the city of Vienna. But when our great struggle for national existence commenced he sundered the thousand ties that bound him to home, friends and his native land, to battle with us in the cause of freedom and constitutional liberty. Arriving on our shores he made known his intentions to the War Department, and was commissioned First Lieutenant in the Second New Jersey cavalry, in which organization he served honorably and bravely until captured, early on General Grant's famous campaign against Richmond.

While a prisoner at Columbia he received intelligence .that his elder brother, who succeeded to the estate and title of his father (some years deceased) ,had departed this life, and the title of Count and the ownership of the estate had thereby fell to him.

As all communications to the prisoners were examinedby the rebel officials in charge, the letter bringing the above intelligence to Lieutenant Von Braiday, also informed the command-ant of the prison that he had a "real live Count " in his keeping, and that worthy immediately came in the pen, and sought an interview with the Count, and expressed. himself as very sorry that he had not been before informed of his position and standing in society, and also insisted that he should no longer remain in prison, but go out and live as a guest at his house until exchanged. The Count, disdaining the proffered hospitality of one who thought it beneath him to treat civily a plain, simple soldier, although a man - the image of the Creator - and pay such obsequiousness to wealth and station, replied, that where he was, he knew he had nearly eleven hundred friends, while if he went outside he would not find one whom he could willingly call such, and therefore, preferred remaining with his fellow prisoners and share their lot.

Captain L. passing by the Count, on one occasion, when he was industriously engaged cutting and splitting wood, with which to kindle a fire to boil his corn meal, enquired of him where he learned the art of chopping? He replied, "In ze prison, to be sure - I no mind him much - but ze washing, Oh! by gar! Why do za no pay ze wash-woman more mone?" The Count's experience, washing his dirty shirt, had brought conviction to his mind that that portion of the laboring population, who take care of our wrist bands, collars, and "dickeys" are poorly paid for their services. After my escape, and while in the city of Washington, I met the Count for the last time, he was then making preparations to sail for Europe, and a few days afterwards departed for his native land, to enjoy his rich heritage of titles, honor, and wealth, and" long may he wave."

LIEUTENANT E. N. REED

This gallant young officer yielded up his life endeavoring to escape from the tortures of southern prisons, in which his courage and powers of endurance, for seventeen months, had struggled with death, but were at last baffled by that scourge of mankind, yellow fever.

At our country's first call for troops to suppress the great rebellion of the nineteenth century, he volunteered as a private in the Third regiment Ohio Volunteer Infantry, in which organization he was known as a faithful and honorable soldier, and was, immediately after the battle of Perryville, promoted to a Lieutenancy.

He was with his regiment on Colonel Streight's expedition in the spring of 1863, through Northern Alabama and Georgia, and in one of the series of engagements of that command with General Forrest's cavalry, received a severe wound in the hip, and fell into the hands of the enemy, who suffered him to lay several days without medical aid or treatment of any kind. In this miserable condition he was thrown into a wagon and for many miles was hauled over a rough, mountainous country, to the railroad at Huntsville, Alabama, where, with many other prisoners, he was packed into a dilapidated old stock car, and started en route for Richmond and incarcerated in the Libby with the other Federal officers. For want of medical attention he suffered here for several months, and while in this painful condition, for a mere imaginary breach of the severe prison regulations, he was thrust into one of the everlasting dungeons in the basement of Libby, where, with no bed but the bare floor, and without a morsel of anything to eat, he was kept for forty-eight hours, his wound at the same time running so as to require frequent washing and dressing. Surviving his wound, ill treatment and the vicissitudes of prison life, he was still with us up to the time we left Charleston, and the morning we started from that city to Columbia he escaped from the guard before getting aboard the train, and sought refuge in an old, uninhabited building in the suburbs of the town. While concealed in this place, watching an opportunity to leave the city and get through to our lines, he was taken with a severe attack of yellow fever - which was then raging in Charleston. It soon exhausted his enfeebled system, and alone, with neither friend or foe to minister to his dying wants, his spirit departed its tenement of clay, and winged its way to the Creator who gave it, adding another to the long list of noble victims, that now sleep in unknown graves beneath the Southern sky, and whose spirits should haunt to the brink of the unquenchable lake, Jefferson Davis and his fiendish co-laborers.

FLINN AND SAWYER

On the sixth of July, 1863, one of the most solemn and deeply interesting ceremonies transpired in Libby Prison that I have ever witnessed. All of the Federal officers of the rank of Captain, (seventy-eight in number,) held as prisoners of war at that time by the rebel authorities, were drawn up in line in one of the rooms on the lower floor, and an order read to them from General Winder to Major Turner, in which the latter officer was directed to select two Captains of the United States army, from among the number he held in confinement, for immediate execution, in retaliation for two rebel officers hung by order of General Burnside. This information produced an instant change on the countenances of the officers whose fate it so much concerned. When first called into line, they stepped out with exuberant spirits, and pleasing anticipations of exchange, home and freedom; but now hilarity was cast aside, and a calm stern resolve to meet, heroic and manfully, whatever fate might befall them in the just cause to which they had dedicated their stout hearts and strong arms, and, if need be, their lives, beamed from the face of each.

The picture was one well worthy the pencil of a Vernet. On a small table, in the center of the circle, formed by the seventy-eight gallant officers, on which was placed a box which contained their names, written on separate slips of paper. At one end of the table, haughty and egotistical, and with a satisfied air, as if the occasion was one productive of pleasure, stood Major Thomas P. Turner, commandant of the prison; at the other, the good old white-haired Chaplain of the Ninth Maryland Infantry, who had been designated by the prisoners to draw two slips of paper from the box, and those whose names were written thereon were to be the doomed men. Solemnly and breathlessly one is drawn, and each, feeling that his life or death depended on it, anxiously awaited the announcement. It is Henry W. Sawyer, Capt. of the First New Jersey Cavalry; all eyes are turned towards him, and a slight commotion ensues, but not a word or exclamation is heard. Again the old Chaplain thrusts his hand in the box; all is silent as death, while from the paper drawn he reads – Captain John Flinn, of the Fifty-First Indiana Volunteer Infantry. The ceremony ended, the doomed men were conducted to General Winder's headquarters for an interview with that officer. He most shamefully cursed and abused them, and notified them that they would be executed within ten days.

A Yankee in Rebel Prisons

After the old gray-haired traitor had exhausted his vocabulary of abusive epithets, he ordered the prisoners back to the Libby to be placed in the dungeon in the basement of that institution, there to be kept until the day of their execution.

Soon as a knowledge of the circumstances were known to our Government, Brigadier General W. F. Lee, of the rebel army, and Captain Winder, son of General John H. Winder, who our authorities held as prisoners of war, were placed in close confinement as hostages for the safety of Flinn and Sawyer, and the rebel authorities notified that if their lives were destroyed, Lee and Winder would be immediately executed in retaliation. This prompt action on the part of our Government had the desired effect - the execution of Flinn and his companion in misfortune was indefinitely deferred, though they were, for a long time, kept in the unhealthy dungeon before spoken of.

They were finally released and placed on the same footing as the other prisoners, and in March, 1864, exchanged for the same officers whom our authorities held for their safety.

The conduct and bearing of these officers (especially that of Captain Flinn,) while the sentence of death hung over their heads, was heroic, calm and dignified. They had grappled with death on many fields of bloody carnage, and in their country's cause they could meet him with firmness, even on that machine of infamy the gallows.

At the time they were confined in the cell, Captain Flinn's health was very poor, yet he was not furnished with anything in the shape of bedding, nor with food fit even for a well man to eat, and, as a consequence, like many other victims of my acquaintance who were there confined, it became seriously and permanently impaired. May his tormentors receive their just reward!

A Yankee in Rebel Prisons

MAJOR B. C. G. REED

Among the many young and gallant spirits who have sealed with their lives their devotion to our Government, none, perhaps, are more worthy of our remembrance and gratitude than the subject of this sketch.

He was among the number of those gallant hearts who bared their breasts to resist the first shock of the rebellion. Enlisting in the Third regiment of Ohio Volunteers, early in the spring of 1861, he served with honor and distinction in the Western Virginia campaigns during the :first year of the war, and for meritorious service was advanced to the grade of Captain. His regiment, forming a part of Colonel Streight's memorable expedition to the rear of Bragg's army, in the spring of 1863, it was his misfortune, along with the whole command, to fall into the hands of the enemy a prisoner of war. His restless and ardent temperament could ill brook the close confinement to which he had to submit, consequently his imaginative and fertile brain was constantly inventing schemes for escape, but iron-grated windows, shackles, hand-cuffs and rebel bayonets, for a long while baffled every effort. His first attempt was with Colonel Streight from Libby Prison in December, 1863, which, as has been shown in another part of this work, was nipped in the bud by the treachery of the guard, who, for a compensation, had agreed to let them pass out.

Soon after being released from the cell, where he was confined with Colonel Streight twenty-one days, on corn-bread and water, as a punishment for the attempted escape, he was selected and sent to Salisbury, North Carolina, in irons, and there placed in close confinement as a hostage for the safety of a rebel officer in the hands of the United States authorities, and against whom were serious charges of conduct not warranted by the rules of war.

A Yankee in Rebel Prisons

From Salisbury, Captain Reed made several efforts to escape, and, on two occasions, succeeded in getting to within a few miles of our troops in East Tennessee, but was, each time, hunted down with blood-hounds, recaptured, and taken back to prison. The sixth and last attempt, and which proved successful, was from the railroad train at Charleston, when we first arrived at that city from Macon, and was as follows:

During one of his expeditions from Salisbury penitentiary, he procured a suit of rebel gray, and, attired in this, he slipped from the car in which he had been riding, and passing along the line of guards stationed around the train, he selected one he thought would be a good subject on whom to practice a "Yankee trick," and endeavored to engage him in conversation, but the guard, supposing him from his dress, to be a resident of the city, ordered him outside the lines, with the remark that neither himself nor the prisoners were allowed to converse with the prisoners. This was just what the adventurous Captain wanted, and, therefore, did not wait for the order to be repeated, though, to keep up the delusion, he started off seemingly reluctantly, and looking in a manner that the guard thought meant vengeance on him for so rudely ordering him away.

Losing himself among the crowd of idle curiosity seekers collected around the depot, to see the Yankee officers, he wended his way to a place of security, where he remained concealed until a dark stormy night gave him an opportunity of passing in a small rowboat down the Ashley river into Charleston harbor, and by the rebel picket boats, and in his frail craft finally reached Sullivan's Island, where he was among friends and under the starry folds of the old flag.

Seldom has such energy, bravery and perseverance been displayed in the pursuit of any one object as by Captain Reed in efforts to gain his liberty, and his comrades were all rejoiced when fate crowned his bravery and energy with success,

Shortly after his arrival at his home in Zanesville, Ohio, he was honored by Governor Brough by an appointment to the Majority of the One Hundred and Seventy-Fourth regiment of Ohio Volunteer Infantry, in which organization he soon endeared himself to both officers and men by his soldierly qualities and genial disposition, But the grim monster, Death, ever envious of noble victims, had already marked him for his own, and, on the seventh of' December, 1864, in the battle on the Wilkinson turnpike, near Murfreesboro, Tennessee, while bravely discharging his duties, the gallant Reed fell mortally wounded, and soon his noble spirit winged its way to the realms of immortality! Thus passed from earth to heaven a noble, lofty soul. Thus our country lost a brave defender, parents an affectionate son, and brother-soldiers a gallant comrade.

In commemoration of his name and gallant services, the following was issued by Major General Thomas, in whose department our heroic friend was serving when he received his death-wound:

"Headquarters, Department of the Cumberland,
Nashville, Tennessee, June 19th, 1865,
General Order, No. 43.

In accordance with the time-honored custom in the United States army, and as an appropriate tribute to the memory of some of our brave comrades whose spirits passed away amid the din of battle, or who died from wounds received in action, or from no less fatal disease contracted in the camp, it is ordered that their names be given to the defensive works of Nashville, which shall stand, for long years to come, fit monuments to their valor and devotion to their country.

VIII. The work on Charlotte turnpike, and the battery between the Charlotte and Harding turnpikes, is named *Battery Reed,* in honor of Major B. C. G. Reed, One Hundred and Seventy-Fourth regiment of Ohio Volunteer Infantry, who was killed in the battle on the Wilkinson turnpike, near Murfreesboro, Tennessee, December seventh, 1864."

His character was of a type which eminently adapted him to the profession of the soldier. He was brave and daring even to rashness, and his virtues were many, while his faults were few. His genial disposition and urbane deportment rendered his conquest of the affections of others easy. The enthusiasm and earnestness of his noble nature enlisted him in the cause in which he fell, as one of its warmest and most zealous advocates.

"To know him was to love him," but to appreciate him, an association of mature growth was necessary. Had he escaped the stern decree which terminated his hopes, his usefulness, and his life; Fame would have wrought for him a chaplet of her choicest flowers.

Noble Spirit, gallant soldier, true friend! green be thy grave and memory! Fare thee well !

THE END.

A Yankee in Rebel Prisons

www.ingramcontent.com/pod-product-compliance
Lightning Source LLC
Chambersburg PA
CBHW031312150426
43191CB00005B/188